Fed By Design

By Glenni Lorick, IBCLC

Fed By Design

ISBN 978-0-9984882-2-6

Copyright © 2023 Glenni Lorick

Published by Inspired Design & Graphics

Table of Contents

Introduction and Acknowledgements

Because I don't particularly enjoy long introductions in books, but I always feel compelled to read the introduction if the author saw fit to write one, I will keep this short and sweet! As you will see in the pages ahead, breastfeeding is the perfect design of a loving Creator. I have been passionate about this topic ever since my first child was born almost 35 years ago and I switched career paths from teaching high school English to teaching moms how to nurture their babies.

The path to publication for Fed By Design has been long and involved, but I am confident that this is the time and manner of publication that the Father has ordained. My prayer for you, sweet reader, is that you can view each chapter as a conversation with a trusted friend who has walked this path with countless young mothers just like you. I pray that you will be able to relate to the moms in each chapter, and that their struggles will help you as you navigate your own breastfeeding journey.

I want to thank several people who have been instrumental in bringing this book to fruition. It has been a 12 year labor of love! First I want to thank Martha Sears who took the time over 10 years ago to painstakingly read my manuscript and call me with her honest feedback. Her input meant more than she will ever know this side of Heaven! I'm also very thankful to Glenda Dickerson who has been a friend and encourager throughout the years. I owe a deep debt of gratitude to Ellise Adams because she saw the spark in me that would end up becoming an IBCLC, encouraged me to write and trusted me to design curriculum when I was just getting started in the field of lactation nearly 30 years ago.

The Lord has brought some amazing encouragers into my life in recent years. Michelle Trossclair, the founder of A Nurturing Moment, a breastfeeding and maternity boutique in Huntsville,

AL, helped me get back into lactation when we returned from Peru. She eventually sold me A Nurturing Moment. Regina Woodley is a dear friend, colleague and so much more. She bought A Nurturing Moment when I was ready to retire from business ownership. More than that, though, Regina generously supported the publication of this book. Her generosity has helped bring us to this point. Finally, Tiffany Martin, the founder of The DandeLion House ministry in Huntsville has become one of my dearest friends, closest confidants and my partner in every aspect of ministry through The MOM Foundation.

I prayed several years ago for a close female friend. The Lord answered that prayer dramatically by bringing Tiffany into my life. Then shortly afterward he brought my Hot Coals sisters to me. This group of ladies loves Jesus and each other! We meet on Tuesdays to share and pray, and I would not be who I am today without the spiritual growth I have experienced because of Rita, Paula, Cheryl, Jana, Ellen, Becky and Nicole. I love you so much!!

Nearly 39 years ago I said "I do" to my best friend, my media naranja, the love of my life, Keith. It has been a fantastic journey that the Father has given us, and I praise God every day for my pastor-husband and for the four amazing children He gave us. Sarah, Daniel, Anna and John Carl live and breathe in the pages of this book because I honed my breastfeeding craft through the four of them! My grandsons Nicholas and Jackson were also blessed to have been lovingly breastfed by their mamas.

Finally, thank you to Angel Gatrey of TQR Imagery for the gorgeous cover photograph. And thank you to Greg Lane of Inspired Graphics and Publications for his invaluable assistance in preparing this book for publication. All glory, praise and honor for anything good that comes from this book belong to my Lord Jesus Christ!

Chapter 1

Eve, Sarah and Mary –
A Biblical Basis for Breastfeeding

"You will drink the milk of nations and be nursed at royal breasts. Then you will know that I, the LORD, am your Savior, your Redeemer, the Mighty One of Jacob."

– Isaiah 60:16 (NIV)

The young mother gazes contentedly at her newborn son as he takes his first meal at her breast. The long day of traveling has taken its toll on her. As she looks up, her eyes meet those of her loving husband. He has been such a source of strength for her during the last months. Brilliant starlight streams through a chink in the rustic stable roof illuminating the beautiful baby as he stops suckling for a moment and looks up at his mother's tender smile. Mary treasures that moment and will remember it 33 years later when that dear Son is suffering on a cruel Roman cross.

A host of artists have sought to depict the precious bond that existed between the infant Savior and his mother Mary. Pictures from the Renaissance typically depict a chubby, happy baby contentedly feeding at his mother's breast. Often in these pictures both mother and child have a halo, or angels hover around them. Certainly there is no Biblical basis for the halo, and it is doubtful that angels flew around every time Jesus nursed. Nevertheless, the artists did get one particularly important thing right: Jesus was lovingly and tenderly breastfed by his mother.

In the Roman world of that time breastmilk substitutes made and marketed by large pharmaceutical firms obviously did not exist. So Mary didn't have much choice. However, Mary didn't just breastfeed Jesus for lack of a better alternative. To Mary's Jewish mind, nurturing her infant at her breast was part of God's wonderful design for mothers and babies – a design that has not changed in the 2000 years since Jesus walked on this earth.

Eve

At the dawn of creation when Eve brought forth her first son Cain, she instinctively knew that God had designed her body to provide the food he needed. She had seen the various mammals God created give birth and nurse their young. Both Eve and her children experienced the many benefits that breastfeeding provides. We know about three of her children: Cain, Abel and Seth. All grew to healthy manhood after beginning life nursing according to God's design.

Sarah

While the Bible doesn't say anything specifically about Jesus or Cain nursing, it does talk specifically about the breastfeeding relationship between several mothers and children. The first is Sarah. Although she had been a stunningly beautiful young woman, she had been infertile – a tremendous stigma in Mesopotamia where fertility was equated with the blessing of the gods. Nevertheless, God has made a promise: Sarah will bear Abraham a son. When he is 100 years old, and she is 90, she gives birth to Isaac, the son God had promised.

Look at Sarah's expression of joy in Genesis 21:6-7, "God has made laughter for me; everyone who hears will laugh with me… Who would have said to Abraham that Sarah would nurse children? Yet I have borne him a son in his old age." She specifically focuses on her motherly role of feeding her infant son. Obviously, she took great delight in being able to breastfeed little Isaac. Then in the next verse we read about Isaac's weaning. The Hebrew word used here means "to deal fully or adequately with." (Strong's 1580) History indicates that weaning took place around the age of 3. Isaac was old enough to understand this very important rite of passage, and his father made a big feast in honor of this step in Isaac's life.

Jochebed

The next breastfeeding mother we read about is Jochebed, the mother of Moses. We read in Exodus 2 that she kept him hidden for the first three months of his life. Part of her strategy was certainly to keep him quiet. The best way to keep a baby quiet is to keep him comfortable, full and content. Undoubtedly she realized that nursing him when he first showed the beginning signs of being hungry was vitally important.

Imagine how difficult it must have been when he was three months old, and she realized that she could no longer keep him hidden. Jochebed put her beautiful infant son to her breast and watched his rhythmic sucking. Surely tears filled her eyes as she thought this might be the last time she ever nursed him. When he was sleeping the contented sleep of a full baby, she tenderly placed him in the little waterproof basket she had so lovingly made. As she placed him into the river, she knew that the LORD God would protect him.

Just a short time later her older daughter, Miriam, came running into the crude hut where they lived as slaves with the incredible news that the princess herself had found him. Furthermore, Miriam had volunteered Jochebed to serve as the infant's wet nurse. In Egyptian culture, the value of breastmilk was widely understood, and children were normally nursed for about three years. Jochebed knew that serving as a wet nurse in the royal family was a high honor indeed, and she surely praised the God of Israel for preserving her son and allowing her to continue mothering him. It was during these first years at his mother's breast that Moses learned the truth about the God of Israel – a truth that no amount of indoctrination in the beliefs and culture of Egypt could erase from his soul.

Hannah

A third mother we read about in Scripture who breastfed is Hannah. Like Sarah, Hannah was unable to conceive early in her marriage. The grief caused by her infertility is evident as she weeps before the Lord in I Samuel 1:10. Through the priest Eli, God encourages her. It appears that within a year Hannah has given birth to Samuel. That year when her husband Elkanah goes to Shiloh to sacrifice to the Lord, Hannah doesn't accompany him. Instead she tells him, "I will not go up until the child is weaned; then I will bring him, that he may appear before the LORD and stay there forever." (I Samuel 1:22) Many Biblical scholars think that Samuel was probably between three and five when Hannah weaned him.

During those first priceless years, Hannah devoted herself to mothering Samuel. Although it is almost impossible for a modern Christian mother to imagine giving her four or five year old child to someone else to raise, Hannah had made a vow to the Lord. Samuel had an incredibly special purpose in God's plan, and his mother understood that. From his first days of feeding at her breast, she had been singing to him about the LORD God. As he began to talk, she taught him how to communicate with the God of the Universe. In short, she had spent his first years preparing Samuel for the mighty purpose God had for his life.

BREASTFEEDING IMAGERY IN SCRIPTURE

The writers of Scripture understood that the image of a mother nursing her infant was a powerful representation of God's nurturing care for his people. In both the Old and New Testaments we see word pictures designed to portray all that is involved in that very special relationship between a mother and her nursing child.

Isaiah 66:10-13

To those who loved God it seemed as if He had forsaken them.

Surely Judah had sinned greatly against the Lord; nevertheless, God had not forgotten them. In Isaiah 66 God reassures His people that He has not forsaken them; He promises that He will restore Jerusalem once again with these words:

> *Be joyful with Jerusalem and rejoice for her, all you who love her; Be exceedingly glad with her, all you who mourn over her. That you may nurse and be satisfied with her comforting breasts, That you may suck and be delighted with her bountiful bosom. For thus says the LORD, "Behold, I extend peace to her like a river, And the glory of the nations like an overflowing stream; And you will be nursed, you will be carried on the hip and fondled on the knees. As one whom his mother comforts, so I will comfort you; And you will be comforted in Jerusalem."*

– Isaiah 66:10-13

The mental picture created by these words evokes the intimacy between mother and child. The word used for "nurse" is yanaq which is a primary root meaning "to suck." (Strong's 3243) Interestingly, the word used for "suck" is a different word -- matsats which literally means "to drain out." (Strong's 4711) The image here is of a baby emptying its mother's breasts. The words for "bountiful bosom" are ziz kabod. Ziz is a relatively obscure word meaning "abundance or fullness" (Strong's 2123b); while kabod can mean abundance, but has the connotation of honor or glory (Strong's 3519b). Breastfeeding a child is a part of what makes a woman glorious – isn't that incredible? When you put your baby to your breast, you are reflecting the glory of the One who designed you to nurture your little one.

However, far more than just milk transfer is going on in Isaiah's wonderful image. The mother, Jerusalem, is filled with peace. It is noteworthy that the hormones prolactin and oxytocin which are responsible for milk production and release are also noted for their tranquilizing effect. A close bond exists between mother and child in this passage as the mother carries him on her hip and plays with him in her lap. The Heavenly Father shows His compassion for his people as He promises to comfort them just like a mother comforts her child.

Psalms

A couple of Psalms make reference to the mother-infant nursing relationship. First in Psalm 8:2 we read these words of David:

> *From the mouth of infants and nursing babes You have established strength Because of Your adversaries, To make the enemy and the revengeful cease.*

As David considers the majesty of God's creation, he recognizes that even the very young can offer praise to God. A mother who sings the Scriptures to her child while she is nursing is filling his little heart with tools he will need to face adversities down the road.

In Psalm 22:9-10 David speaks of God's sovereignty in bringing him to faith:

> *Yet you brought me out of the womb; you made me trust in you even at my mother's breast. From birth I was cast upon you; from my mother's womb you have been my God.*

A mother can have no greater delight than seeing her children follow the Lord. Perhaps one of the most important reasons to breastfeed and practice other aspects of attachment parenting is found in verse 9. As mothers we are always teaching our children from the moment they are born. One of the first things we teach is that they can trust us. A baby learns the wonderful lesson of trust when his loving mother responds to his hunger cues and feeds him, or when she offers him her breast to comfort him in the midst of a distressing situation. David's mother clearly responded to him like a good Jewish mother and taught him lessons about trust that he carried with him throughout his life.

New Testament Examples

Two New Testament authors use breastfeeding imagery to express their thoughts. The first is Paul. In I Thessalonians 2:7 he says, "But we proved to be gentle among you, as a nursing mother tenderly cares for her own children." Some who had come to know Christ under Paul's ministry in Thessalonica were now being persecuted, and Paul sought to encourage them in this letter. He describes his bond with them in terms of a nursing mother and her child. What a poignant picture!

The next New Testament writer to allude to breastfeeding is Peter, who wrote to believers scattered throughout the world of that day. His purpose was to encourage holy living. In chapter 2 he tells them, "Like newborn babies, long for the pure milk of the word, so that by it you may grow in respect to salvation, if you have tasted the kindness of the Lord." (vv. 2-3) This simile may bring a smile to a new mother's face as she thinks about how eagerly her baby searches for her breast at feeding time.

Another interesting note here is the meaning of the word "pure." In the Greek it is adolos which has the idea of "guileless or genuine." (Strong's 97) There is no substitute for the pure milk of God's Word in the life of a new believer. Christian books can be helpful, but they can't take the place of God's Word. In the same way, although infant formulas may offer important nutrients to an infant, they can never match up to the real thing. As we will see in the next chapter, breastmilk has so many elements that act in specific ways to enhance a baby's development, that no man-made substitute can ever fully replace it.

A Special Blessing

As this chapter opened we were peeking in on Mary nursing the infant Jesus. Over 30 years later, an anonymous woman in the crowd made a very interesting comment. The Bible tells us she "raised her voice" and cried out these words: "Blessed is the womb that bore You and the breasts at which You nursed." (Luke 11:27) This woman recognized the truth that motherhood is indeed a tremendous privilege and blessing. Like Mary, Eve, Jochebed, Sarah and Hannah, you have the opportunity to give your child the very best possible start in life by feeding him according to God's perfect design as laid out in His Word.

Chapter 2

God's Wonderful Design for Feeding Your Baby –
How Breastfeeding Works

"For You formed my inward parts; You wove me in my mother's womb. I will give thanks to You, for I am fearfully and wonderfully made: Wonderful are Your works, And my soul knows it very well."

– *Psalm 139:13-14*

LaShonda was nursing her newborn daughter when I entered her hospital room. "I don't think I have any milk, Miss Glenni," she said tearfully. I looked closely at baby Jeannette who was latched on and suckling contentedly, and I heard the little sighs that indicated her swallows.

"Listen," I responded, "do you hear those little swallows? She's doing so well! She's getting the colostrum that she needs, and you are both on your way to a great nursing relationship! Just be sure to get lots of skin-to-skin contact and nurse as often as she will. The more time you have her skin-to-skin, the more prolactin and oxytocin your body will produce." When I called to check on them a week later, LaShonda told me that her daughter was nursing like a champ and getting milk drunk at every feed.

When you hold your infant daughter in your arms, you are holding a special creation of God whose genes carry the blueprint for her to someday nurse your grandchild. God has designed women to nurture their offspring. We begin by nurturing our babies for nine months inside the womb. However, our role as nurturing provider is just getting underway when we give birth. The hormonal reactions that take place during the birth process prompt a woman's body to begin producing milk. Even mothers who don't take advantage of this wonderful opportunity will experience the breast fullness that comes with the onset of milk production. Breastfeeding is like a beautifully orchestrated ballet in which both you and your baby have leading roles.

MOM'S ROLE

The female breast is truly a marvel. It is composed of many milk glands or alveoli connected by a system of ducts. If you picture a tree with its trunk, its limbs and its branches, you will have an idea of how each lobe in the breast looks. Picture the trunk ending with the nipple openings. Typically women have between 15 and 20 of these lobes in each breast. Often they will notice that milk shoots out from several of these openings at once.

In early adolescence most girls notice changes in their breasts. The network of ducts and alveoli that will someday produce milk is beginning to grow. When she begins to menstruate, a girl will notice increased growth and changes in her breasts. Actually with each ovulatory cycle the hormone progesterone causes growth in the duct tissue. Research indicates that new alveoli and ducts continue to form until a woman is around 35. (Riordan, 82) Some girls have larger breasts than others, but breast size has absolutely nothing to do with the ability to breastfeed.

It is during pregnancy that the breasts change in preparation for breastfeeding. The hormones estrogen, progesterone and prolactin produced during the pregnancy cause the first stage of growth early on. In fact, one of the classic symptoms of pregnancy is tender breasts. That tenderness is related to the rapid proliferation of new ducts and alveoli. You will also notice that your areola (the dark pigmented circle around your nipple) gets larger and looks like it has little pimples on it. They aren't really pimples; they are called Montgomery Glands, and they secrete a lubricant that helps keep the breast and nipple healthy. They also smell like amniotic fluid to your newborn and help draw baby in for that first feed.

In the last half of pregnancy, your breasts begin to secrete colostrum. Colostrum is the nutritious first milk that your baby will receive. After you give birth and deliver the placenta, the sharp drop in estrogen and progesterone will signal your body that it is time to begin producing milk. Two especially important hormones are responsible for successful breastfeeding.

Prolactin

The word prolactin comes from a Latin root meaning "milk." The prefix "pro" means "for." So the hormone prolactin is responsible for the production of human milk. During pregnancy this hormone plays an important role in the growth and development of the breasts. It is primarily produced in the anterior pituitary gland and controlled by the hypothalamus. Every time your baby nurses, your prolactin levels double; they peak between 15 minutes and an hour after you first put your baby to the breast. The more frequently you nurse, the more milk your body will produce. It has been compared to a "demand and supply" situation. The baby demands, and your breasts supply! Some researchers have concluded that frequent nursing in the first ninety-six hours of your baby's life actually makes your breasts more receptive to prolactin resulting in increased milk production. (Riordan, 88)

Prolactin has been called "The Mothering Hormone" because of the effect is has on a woman's emotional outlook. Studies have shown that prolactin increases motherly feelings. It also seems to have a calming and relaxing effect on mothers. Some researchers even think that it may help to prevent or minimize the "baby blues" that so many mothers experience around the third day post-partum. However, not all scientists agree on this point.

Gloria (note that all the names of mothers and babies have been changed, but the stories are all true) was a very intense person who was easily flustered. When she had any kind of deadline, she would fly into a frenzy. However, when she gave birth to Sally, her husband noticed some dramatic changes. Every time she would nurse, she would become very tranquil. In fact, during the entire two years that she nursed Sally, she was far calmer than she had been before. Gloria explained that she felt a sense of well-being the moment she sat down in her rocking chair to nurse. Prolactin and its companion hormone, oxytocin, made a real difference in her state of mind.

Oxytocin

This wonderful hormone which is produced in the posterior pituitary gland is responsible for the release of milk. It is released in direct response to a baby's suckling and causes the smooth muscle cells around each of the alveoli in the breast to release the milk into the network of ducts. Many mothers experience a tingling, a sense of pressure, or even a sharp pain when this milk ejection reflex (MER) occurs. On the other hand, some mothers don't feel anything, but they may notice that milk begins leaking out of the other breast. Often a mother may experience let-down (the letting down of milk that occurs with the MER) even before she puts her baby to the breast. Oxytocin is very receptive not only to physical stimuli but also to psychological stimuli.

Oxytocin has many beneficial effects for the mother. In the first hours and days after birth, it causes her uterus to contract. In fact, mothers in the hospital are given synthetic oxytocin, called pitocin, to cause the uterus to contract in order to prevent hemorrhage. Early postpartum mothers often notice cramps or even strong labor-like pains when they begin to nurse. This effect is especially noticeable for women who are having a second, third or fourth baby. In fact, with each baby, the cramps become a little more intense. The only time I had any birth-related medication with my third and fourth babies was when I was breastfeeding after giving birth. Then I gladly accepted some pain relievers to alleviate the discomfort!

Another notable effect of oxytocin is its ability to produce relaxation. It is recognized as a stress-reducing hormone. It has also been described as a love-inducing hormone which, when coupled with prolactin, produces an incredibly strong attachment between mother and baby.

It is truly amazing how God designed the hormonal mechanisms for lactation in such a way that mothers would have psychological and emotional incentives to keep on breastfeeding their babies through the often difficult first days. However, the hormones adrenaline and cortisol which are caused by emotional distress or other stresses in a mother's life actually block the release of oxytocin and can inhibit the production of prolactin as well.

Nancy was worried because baby Seth didn't seem to be regaining his birth weight very quickly. She didn't show any signs of experiencing let-down; Seth was fussy at the breast, and Nancy always seemed extremely nervous. When I first went to her house, she was in tears. After praying with her, I began to share Scripture to encourage her: "I can do all things through Him who strengthens me" (Phil. 4:13) and "Do not fear, for I am with you; do not anxiously look about you, for I am your God; I will strengthen you, surely I will help you, surely I will uphold you with My righteous right hand." (Is. 41:10) Then I urged her to close her eyes and picture her baby nursing contentedly because her body was producing an abundance of milk. As her emotional distress subsided (and the adrenaline in her system diminished), she was able to begin experiencing the effects of prolactin and oxytocin. Within days Nancy was making plenty of milk and Seth had not only regained his birth weight but was steadily growing.

BABY'S ROLE

The most important thing the baby does is suck, so it is crucial that he do it correctly! When a baby latches on to his mother's breast, he should have his mouth wide open. His tongue should be covering his bottom gum, and he should take as much of the areola into his mouth as possible. Generally an infant will take 1 ½ to 2 inches of nipple and areola into his mouth. His tongue will stroke the nipple beginning at the base of the nipple where the milk ducts collect pooled milk and move the milk in the breast forward to the nipple opening. As the milk leaves the breast it collects in the back of his mouth which causes him to swallow. The rhythmic cycle of sucks and swallows indicates that he is getting the milk his little body needs to grow.

When he first latches on, a baby will have a burst of rapid sucks with a couple of swallows. Usually within a few seconds his mother will experience let-down, and one of two things will happen. He will either begin a rhythmic pattern of slower sucks and swallows, or he will pull away from the breast because he can't handle all the milk he's getting at one time. Some mothers do have an overly strong MER, and they must learn how to help their babies cope with this. Specific techniques for dealing with a strong MER are found in chapter 3.

When baby first latches on, if Mom hasn't fed for a while the baby will get milk that is more watery; however, as baby continues to nurse, the milk gradually increases in fat content as the fatty cells lining the alveoli are shed. If the breast is less full because baby has nursed more recently, the first milk he gets will likely be higher in fat content. Mom may notice that part way through the feed baby begins rhythmically sucking and swallowing (some moms would call it gulping) once again. Sometimes the first more watery milk is referred to as foremilk and the fattier milk is referred to as hind-milk. But it is important to realize that the breast really isn't making two different kinds of milk. It is more like a continuum – the longer baby suckles, the more fatty milk he pulls from the breast. That's why it is so important to let baby completely finish nursing on the first side before offering him the second side.

The majority of breastfeeding problems occur because the baby is not nursing correctly. It is vitally important to make sure that he is latched on well and is sucking correctly. Mothers who are worried that this isn't happening need to contact a lactation consultant for help.

Anne had a beautiful baby girl, Jenna, who wasn't gaining weight well. Anne's nipples were cracked and bleeding when I saw her, but because her breasts were so full, she kept trying to nurse. Initially we used a breastpump to relieve the engorgement and allow her nipples to heal. However, when she did put Jenna back to the breast, Jenna was only getting the nipple in her mouth. We worked with Jenna to get her to open her mouth wider, and Anne learned how to hold her breast properly with her thumb on top and fingers underneath, well away from the areola. When Jenna finally opened her mouth wide, Anne filled it up with her breast. Jenna began sucking and swallowing like she never had before. Within a few days Anne's nipples were completely healed, and Jenna had already begun to show a weight gain.

BENEFITS ABOUND WHEN YOU FOLLOW GOD'S PLAN!

The many benefits of breastfeeding are well documented. Of course the Creator designed it this way. His plan is always perfect, and as we will see, straying from his plan can actually cause problems down the road.

Benefits for Mom

Mothers who breastfeed return to their pre-pregnancy condition more rapidly. The oxytocin causes the uterus to clamp down and return to its normal size more quickly. Breastfeeding mothers burn up extra calories in producing breastmilk, so they don't need to diet to loose those extra pregnancy pounds. Some mothers find that they are in their best physical condition while they are nursing.

Studies have shown a relationship between breastfeeding and reduced rates of osteoporosis as well as breast, uterine, ovarian and endometrial cancers. Furthermore women who were breastfed themselves are at a lower risk for breast cancer, so when you breastfeed your daughter you are giving her extra protection. The longer cumulative time you breastfeed, the more protection you afford yourself. It also reduces your risk for Type 2 diabetes.

Breastmilk is always available, is just the right temperature and doesn't cost a cent. Mothers who formula feed must first spend a small fortune to buy it – especially if they have a baby who can't tolerate the less expensive milk-based formulas. Then they have to mix the formula and heat it to the right temperature. If you have a frantically hungry baby, it must be nerve-wracking to have to wait until that formula is ready! Furthermore, when you breastfeed you don't have to worry about keeping all the bottles and nipples clean and ready to go.

Many mothers don't have menstrual periods while they are exclusively breastfeeding. This effect is known as lactational amenorrhea. There is actually a birth control method known as the lactational amenorrhea method (LAM) which is as effective as the birth control pill. However, mothers can't assume that simply because they are breastfeeding they won't get pregnant. In order for LAM to work a mother must do the following:

- exclusively breastfeed on demand,
- nurse during the night – once baby sleeps through the night the mother's hormone levels change,
- not have had a period. (Kennedy)

Some mothers find that their periods don't return for well over a year, while other mothers begin menstruating again during the baby's first six months. Usually babies begin to eat solid foods around 6 months; LAM is only effective during the time before babies begin to eat other foods.

The American Academy of Pediatrics recommends that infants sleep on their back in a crib or bassinet with a firm mattress in their parents' room (https://pediatrics.aappublications.org/content/138/5/e20162938). An Arm's Reach Cosleeper or Halo Bassinet will allow your baby to be right next to you during the night.

If you do bring baby into your bed to nurse, be sure that you are following the guidelines suggested by Dr. James McKenna of the Nortre Dame Mother-Baby Behavioral Sleep Laboratory. (https://cosleeping.nd.edu/safe-co-sleeping-guidelines/)

Some breastfeeding mothers do prefer to simply snuggle their babies up next to them in bed for nighttime feedings. Traditionally in many cultures this has been the norm, even though in western culture it often is not. However, studies have shown that when babies sleep with their mothers their breathing is better regulated and there is less chance of sleep apnea because they share the same sleep cycles.(Mosko) The decision about where baby will sleep is a very important one and should not be taken lightly. Do your research and make sure that as a couple, you are completely comfortable with your choices.

Mothers generally don't have to worry about giving their babies a cold or bug. When a mother who has a cold or virus nurses her baby she passes antibodies to him through her milk. So breastfed babies tend to pick up fewer illnesses from family members.

Nursing babies know their mothers; they are strongly attached to them, in fact. A breastfed baby recognizes his mother's smell and knows when she is in the room. You will be the center of your baby's world. That is a wonderful place to be during this precious season of life!

Breastfed babies smell good. They have a sweet baby scent that formula fed babies do not have. Even the dirty diapers of breastfed babies have a less offensive odor than those of formula-fed babies. This is a real blessing for a mom who is changing 8 or more diapers a day!

The final benefit for the mother is the certainty that she has given her baby the very best possible start in life. The very first thing that he is learning is trust – and he is learning that at his mother's breast, just like David did!

Benefits for Baby

Breastfed babies have far fewer incidences of ear infections, upper respiratory infections and gastrointestinal infections than their formula fed counterparts. The antibodies found in breastmilk provide protection against more serious illnesses, as well. Research has shown that breastfed babies have less incidence of lymphoma and other childhood cancers. They are also at a lower risk for juvenile diabetes.

Breastmilk is designed to be the perfect food for babies. It is easily digested. It changes as they grow older to meet their changing needs. In fact, it even changes throughout the day. The combination of nutrients and enzymes in breastmilk cannot be duplicated by any artificial formula. In fact, some babies who cannot tolerate either lactose based or soy based formulas are able to thrive on breastmilk. Furthermore, its molecular structure makes it the ideal food for an infant's little intestines.

Research indicates that babies who are breastfed for a year or longer have higher IQ's when all the variables are factored in. Breastmilk contains an enzyme that helps the synapses of the brain to make connections. Some scientists feel like this may be the reason for these findings. Formula companies have added DHA to their products to attempt to replicate this effect. But synthetic DHA is simply not the same as the DHA your body makes.

Children who were breastfed as babies have fewer orthodontic problems. This doesn't mean that breastfed babies won't ever need braces, but breastfeeding does contribute to the proper development of the jaw and teeth.

Breastfed babies have far fewer problems with allergies than formula-fed infants. If either parent has a family history of allergies, it would be unwise NOT to breastfeed. The protection afforded by breastfeeding lasts far beyond the first year of life; in fact, children who were nursed as infants have less incidence of asthma later in life.

Some studies have found a link between breastfeeding and a lower incidence of Sudden Infant Death Syndrome (SIDS). (McKenna)This effect is dramatically increased when parents are non-smokers. Because breastfed babies have lighter sleep cycles, some researchers hypothesize that they are at lower risk for the apnea that might lead to SIDS.

Babies who are nursed according to their cues cry far less than other babies. They are more content and don't need to resort to a frantic cry to get somebody's attention. Furthermore, they are readily comforted at the breast. Usually when my babies would receive their vaccinations, I would already have them nursing. They would pull off for a moment and cry, then go right back to nursing. The nurses often commented on how easily they had been comforted.

Speaking of vaccinations...research indicates that breastfeeding has a positive effect on the way an infant's body responds to the vaccination. They tend to create more antibodies than formula fed children.

Breastmilk contains an amino acid, tryptophan, which helps babies regulate their sleep cycles. This important substance also helps regulate appetite and even seems to affect the perception of pain. Because of the daily variations in breastmilk, tryptophan is most bioavailable in the late evening when infants most need it.

Finally, babies who are breastfed on cue have the privilege of learning from the first day of their lives what it means to be able to trust a caregiver. They aren't forced to wait until a clock says it's time to nurse. They know that Mommy will meet their needs, and they are content, happy and carefree. As they grow older, they will be able to better understand what it means to trust their Heavenly Father.

Chapter 3:

In the Beginning –
Feeding Your Newborn

"And she gave birth to her firstborn son; and she
wrapped Him in cloths, and laid Him in a manger,
because there was no room for them in the inn."– –
– Luke 2:7

It must have been an incredible moment when Mary, lying on a pallet of hay and surrounded by the sounds and smells of a stable, gave birth to the infant Savior. Perhaps the innkeeper's wife attended her, or maybe Joseph was able to find a midwife to be with her. Like her mother and grandmother before her, Mary put Jesus to her breast shortly after he was born. That was the Jewish way. It was the natural thing to do. When his quiet alert state had subsided, and the baby Jesus was slumbering peacefully, she lovingly placed him in the only bed available, a feeding trough where the innkeeper's donkeys and cows took their meals.

When Sarah, my first daughter was born, it was a very different situation. Because I had an epidural and couldn't feel to push with my contractions, it took a couple of hours to push her out. The doctor ended up using forceps, and Sarah swallowed a bit of my blood while she was stuck in the birth canal. After she was born, a nurse whisked her away to the intensive care nursery because they were concerned about the blood she had spit up. Several hours later, around midnight, I finally held my daughter in my arms and nursed her. Our nursing got off to a rough start because neither of us really knew what we were doing. My wonderful lactation consultant gave me lots of help and support both in the hospital and after I got home. Thanks to her, Sarah and I ended up having a long, wonderful nursing relationship.

Ten years later John Carl entered the world in a small birthing center in the suburbs of Lima, Peru. My midwife had helped me give birth in a very comfortable position, and shortly after the cord was cut little Juan Carlitos, as we called him there, was happily nursing at my breast. An hour or so later, after he had fallen into a contented sleep, I was taken to the whirlpool bath that had been drawn for me and was able to completely relax. It was truly an ideal birth.

Choosing where to have your baby

Each time you give birth, it is an unforgettable experience. Some mothers want to avoid an "institutionalized" birth, so they opt to give birth at home or at a birthing center rather than in a hospital. Most health care professionals would agree that it is wise to have access to proper medical care for those very rare times when the unexpected happens. Many mothers like the idea of a birthing center. Often, rather than having an obstetrician attend the delivery, a Certified Nurse Midwife will be with the mother. Because of her training, a CNM provides a different kind of attention than the traditional obstetrician. The CNM remains with the mother throughout her labor, and encourages her to work with her body, instead of making her follow rigid hospital protocol that actually fights against the normal birth process.

Another kind of midwife is the Certified Profesisonal Midwife (CPM). A CPM does not have the same kind of training as a CNM; nevertheless, the profession is regulated, and practitioners do have extensive training in caring for normal pregnancies. A good CPM will also know when a situation is beyond her scope of practice. Generally a CPM will work in a birth center setting or will specialize in home deliveries. If you do choose to have a CPM attend you, be sure that she has a good working relationship with a nearby Ob/Gyn and hospital.

In some regions of the country, it is almost impossible to find a safe place where a CNM or a CPM is delivering. However, you can almost always find a doula. A doula is a woman who stays with you throughout your labor. She has special training to help you labor as comfortably as possible. She also serves as your advocate with the hospital staff, helping to ensure that you get the kind of birth you want. To find a doula go to https://www.dona.org/

Wherever you choose to give birth, it is certain that the more you learn during your pregnancy about the normal birth process, the higher your likelihood is that you will have a normal delivery. When you choose a birth care provider, make sure that he or she understands the things that are important to you in the birth process. Many mothers create a birth plan so that they can have some control over what happens. Pregnancy is not an illness; rather, it is a normal part of a woman's life. Likewise, most babies can be born with a minimum of medical intervention.

Many mothers experience some difficulties breastfeeding their firstborn. Good pre-natal education can make a dramatic difference in a mother's confidence level and in her initial success. One critical factor for breastfeeding success is the support that a new mom is able to receive. The ideal is to find a hospital or birthing center that has received the "Baby Friendly Hospital" designation by WHO/UNICEF. This initiative encourages hospitals to comply with ten steps that have been proven to promote successful breastfeeding. Over 20,000 hospitals worldwide have received this designation from their governments. In the United States we have over 500 facilities designated as Baby Friendly. To find a hospital or birthing center near you that is Baby Friendly, you can follow this link: https://www.babyfriendlyusa.org/for-parents/find-a-baby-friendly-facility/ You will notice that many areas don't have any Baby Friendly facilities within 100 miles or more. One thing that mothers can do is insist that local hospitals implement the steps required to become Baby Friendly. Several states have state-wide initiatives designed to encourage hospitals to have more pro-breastfeeding policies. If you have several hospitals in your area, you would be wise to talk to other mothers, talk to breast-feeding–friendly pediatricians, and actually call each hospital to find out if the staff supports breastfeeding. Some questions to ask include the following:

• What percentage of mothers giving birth in your facility ini-tiates breastfeeding? This percentage should be very high. A hos-pital that is actively encouraging breastfeeding will usually have an 85% or higher initiation rate. However, some large public hospitals have lower rates because of the population they serve. That may not mean they aren't actively encouraging breastfeeding. Before making a final decision ask the remaining questions.

• Do they have a International Board Certified Lactation Con-sultants (IBCLC) on staff? When is a mother seen by a lactation consultant? Are all mothers seen? Can a mother specifically re-quest a visit from the lactation consultant, or is it by referral only?

• If your baby is born on the weekend, will a lactation nurse or a lactation consultant be available to help you?

• Do they encourage rooming-in where your baby remains in your room instead of being cared for separately in the nursery? Are the nurses trained in mother/baby care? Have all the nurses who work on the maternity unit received training in breastfeeding management and support?

• Do they have plenty of extra pillows on hand for nursing mothers, or should you plan to bring your own?

• Are all babies routinely given glucose water? If the answer to this question is yes, then you need to find a different hospital!

• Are breastfed babies given formula without medical indica-tion? Are they routinely given pacifiers? Again, a "yes" here is a bad sign!

• Do they have breastpumps and proper support available in case you or baby experience complications and you have to pump?

• Do they sponsor a breastfeeding support group, or can they recommend community-based groups?

The first time you feed your baby

One of the most important indicators of long-term breast-feeding success occurs during the first 90 minutes after birth. Research shows that the baby's suckling reflex is most intense during the first hour following birth. If babies are allowed to breastfeed during those first critical minutes, they take advantage of this reflex and learn from the beginning how to nurse correctly. (Sinusis and Gagliardi) Skin to skin contact helps to stabilize your baby's breathing, heartbeat, body temperature and blood sugar. Babies who nurse during the first hour of life also have a reduced risk of infant mortality. (Crenshaw)

After your baby is born and the umbilical cord is cut, but before the drops are placed in his eyes and he is examined, ask that he be placed on your stomach with his head almost between your breasts. The pigmentation of the areola and nipple will attract his attention, and you will be surprised to see how he moves toward the breast. Doctors have observed that most healthy term babies, if left in this position, will latch on within an hour of birth. Resist the temptation to rush baby; he will latch on when he's ready. If you try to help him too much, you might actually impede the process. This is a key learning experience for you and your baby.

The distance at which a newborn can see clearly is about 12 inches. Another marvelous aspect of God's special design is the distance from your breast to your face: 12 inches. When you hold him at your breast he can gaze clearly into your loving eyes! Enjoy these first moments of getting to know each other. Your baby is likely to remain in a quiet alert state for about an hour or an hour and a half after he is born. Then he will fall into a contented sleep.

Have a feeding plan

Just as you might have created a birth plan explaining what you want for your birth, you should also create an infant feeding plan. Make sure that your obstetrician and pediatrician both have a copy on file and that the hospital also has a copy. You should also place a copy in the bag that you are planning to take with you to the hospital or birthing center. In your feeding plan you should include the following:

• Your desire to nurse your baby shortly after birth before drops are placed in his eyes and before he is examined. If he is full term and appears healthy, this should not be a problem.

• Instructions that your baby not receive any glucose water or formula during his time in the hospital unless there is a specific medical indication. Healthy babies do not need anything other than breastmilk. Many hospitals used to routinely give babies glucose water to make sure they could swallow properly. However, research has shown that for a breastfed baby this procedure is not necessary.

• Instructions about how often you want to nurse your baby. Ideally a newborn should nurse every couple of hours during the day and at least once during the night. While you are in the hospital is a good time to learn how to feed him on cue. However, if he is a very sleepy baby, he may need to be awakened to nurse. Many hospitals have a healthy baby remain in his mother's room 24 hours a day. Having your baby close to you will help you both get the rest you need!

• Instructions that your baby is not to have any kind of artificial nipple. He does not need a pacifier. If he isn't in your room and begins crying, he should be brought to you. Studies have shown that infants who are given a bottle or pacifier sometimes have difficulty learning to suck properly at the breast. This is known as nipple confusion. If your nipples are small or not very everted, and your baby is given a different firmer nipple, it can be frustrating to baby that your nipple doesn't feel that way. Your baby wants to feel your nipple against the back of his palate, and if all he has experienced is your nipple, he may be just fine. But introducing a firmer nipple can cause baby not to like the way your nipple feels. This can all be avoided by making sure that the only nipple your baby ever has in his mouth for the first weeks is yours!

• You need to indicate where you want your baby to sleep. As noted previously, the best scenario is rooming-in.

• Finally, you need to explain your plan for feeding your baby if, due to complications, he is unable to breastfeed at first. If you want him to still receive your breastmilk, you need to include that as part of your feeding plan and ask that a hospital grade electric breastpump be made available.

Getting it right

Knowing a few specific strategies will help you get off to the right start with your baby. Positioning is one of the single most important factors in preventing sore nipples and in making sure that your baby gets enough to eat. Four of the most common positions are the cradle hold, the reverse cradle hold, the football or underarm hold, and lying down.

In the cradle hold, also known as the Madonna hold, your newborn's head is actually on your forearm at the level of your breast, with your hand supporting his little buttocks. Make sure that his tummy is right up against yours, and he doesn't have to turn his head at all to reach your breast. With your other hand, you will hold the breast in a "C-hold." Your thumb will be on top, and your fingers underneath the breast, well away from the areola. You will find that putting a pillow on your lap underneath him will help you hold him at the right level to reach your breast. Many types of nursing pillows exist; they are wonderful, but a firm bed pillow will accomplish the same thing. The goal is to bring your baby's mouth level with your breast.

In the reverse cradle hold, your newborn's buttocks will rest on your forearm. Your hand will gently cradle the back of his head, providing support for him as he nurses. He will still need to have his tummy right up against to yours. You will use your right hand to support your right breast and your left hand to support your left breast using the C-hold described earlier. It's a good idea to have a pillow underneath baby in this position, too. You will also find that putting an additional pillow underneath your elbow makes it much more comfortable. This position is really ideal for newborns because it provides the head support necessary to help the newborn maintain the nipple in his mouth.

The football hold is aptly named because your newborn is tucked up under your arm just like a football. Begin by placing a pillow next to you and placing your newborn on it. With your forearm you will support his upper body, and your hand will support the base of his head. As your baby grows, you may find that it is helpful to put his little bottom against the back of the chair or bed with his legs pointing up. As with the other holds, your free hand will support the breast in a C-hold. The football hold is wonderful for mothers who have given birth by cesarean. It is also very good for small or premature babies. Often mothers with larger breasts prefer this position. Mothers with sore nipples will also find that switching to this hold relieves the pressure on the sore spots.

Another position that works well for mothers who have had Cesareans is nursing while lying down. You will want to have lots of pillows available. You might put one between your legs, one behind your back, and one up against and under your belly if you've had a C-section. You will lie on one side with your baby on her side facing you, her mouth at the level of your nipple. Place a rolled towel or blanket behind her for support. With your top hand support your breast in a C-hold. You can place your other hand behind baby's head to help offer support if you need to. This is also a wonderful position for nighttime nursing or for taking a nap with your baby.

Latching on

Once you have your baby properly positioned at the breast, you will need to make sure that he latches on correctly. You want to get as much of the nipple and areola in his mouth as possible. It is sort of like feeding him a "breast sandwich." You want to compress your breast tissue with your fingers behind the areola so that he is able to get as much as possible in his mouth. A baby who is properly latched onto his mother's breast will have about 1 ½ - 2 inches from the tip of the nipple in his mouth. He should be cupping the nipple and areola with his tongue. If you feel his bottom gum on your breast, he isn't latched on correctly. Finally, his lips should be flanged like a little rose. Here is a step by step guide to the perfect latch:

• Make sure your baby is positioned correctly and his nose is level with your nipple. Hold your breast with a C-hold where your thumb is on top and your fingers below the breast well back from the areola.

• DO NOT allow him to latch on until his mouth is wide open. If you let him latch on with a half-open mouth, you will end up with very sore nipples.

• Gently rub your nipple just under his nose and wait until he opens his mouth as wide as it will open.

• The instant he opens wide, feed him a breast sandwich by placing as much of your breast as possible in his mouth.

Let-down

Your baby will probably begin to nurse with rapid, shallow sucks. As your milk ejection reflex (let-down) occurs, he will begin a series of slower rhythmic sucks and swallows as described in chapter 2. Some mothers experience such a strong let-down that their babies pull off. If you find that your baby pulls away after a few seconds of sucking, this may very well be the cause. If you experience this problem, you can try to make your milk let down before your baby latches on by applying warm compresses and using a breast pump or manual expression to elicit the milk ejection reflex. You might want to have a towel ready if you're using manual expression and let the milk spray into the towel before letting baby latch on.

Some babies let go of the nipple and start crying because they can't handle the strong influx of milk. If your baby does pull off or even seems to choke a bit on your milk, then the first thing you must do is comfort him. Hold him upright and pat his back until he settles. Then put him back to the breast, and he should be able to nurse without a problem. Another solution that works for some mothers is to hold the baby in more of a vertical position when he is nursing. Some mothers with a strong MER also find it helpful to nurse lying on their backs with the baby stomach to stomach. If you are having problems with an excessively strong MER, it is a good idea to work with a lactation consultant.

Changing breasts

For optimal weight gain it is best for a baby to completely finish nursing on one breast. That way he will get as much fatty milk as possible. After your baby has been nursing for about 5-10 minutes, you may notice that his suck/swallow rhythm slows down. If he seems to be dozing off, you can use the fingers and thumb supporting your breast to gently massage the milk downward toward the nipple. This will cause him to begin sucking again. Usually after about 7-10 minutes will have another let down and once again he will begin a pattern of rhythmic sucks and swallows.

After he has completely finished the first breast, he may just let go by himself. If he doesn't, you need to carefully insert your finger in the corner of his mouth to break the suction before you remove him from the breast. Once you have burped him, if he still seems to want more, you can put him on the other breast.

Burping your baby

Some babies nurse like little barracudas and take in a lot of air. Other babies nurse more slowly like gourmet taste testers and don't gulp air like their barracuda counterparts. Not all breastfed babies will actually burp; however, it's always a good idea to try to see if baby needs to burp. The traditional way to burp a baby is to put him up on your shoulder and pat his back. The mistake that most new parents make is that they are afraid to really do what it takes to get baby to burp.

What you are trying to accomplish here is nothing short of forcing a bubble of air up from your baby's stomach and out his mouth. In order to do that, you must put pressure on that little tummy. One way is to make sure that his tummy is pressing down upon your shoulder (with a burp cloth underneath to catch spit-up milk). Use the hand of the shoulder he is on to support his body by hooking your thumb under his armpit with your hand over his back. With your other hand firmly pat or rub his back.

A second position is sitting on your lap. The palm of one hand will be against his stomach, and with the fingers and thumb you will support his head. With the other hand you will pat or rub his back with an upward motion. Another position that often works is to lay him face down across your lap. Be sure that his tummy is pressing against one of your thighs. Once again, you will pat or rub his back to elicit a burp. Often just moving him from one position to another will cause him to burp. Once he has burped, he may be ready to eat a little bit more. If so, give him the chance to nurse from the other breast for as long as he wants to.

Ending a feeding

Frequently a newborn who has nursed well will fall into a deep sleep at the breast. He will actually let go of the nipple himself. If he does not, you can use the technique mentioned above to remove him. If he has entered into a deep state of sleep, he may sleep for an hour and a half or more. After the first week or so, you will find that he may finish nursing, but not be ready to sleep. As the first month comes to a close, you will find this happening with greater frequency. Take advantage of this time to interact with your baby. Sing to him or read to him. Play with him using a toy that has red and black. Research shows that those colors are especially stimulating for newborns.

The next time you feed your baby, you will start on the opposite breast from the one you started on this feed. If you only nursed on one breast, then you will nurse on the other one next feed. If your baby finished one breast and then nursed some on the other breast, you will start with the breast he ended on. You can put a safety pin on your bra strap to remind you which breast goes first next feeding, or use a bracelet that you move from wrist to wrist.

Home Sweet Home

As we loaded baby Sarah into the infant safety seat that our hospital had given us and took her home to our little house with the freshly painted nursery, I had the surreal sense of watching somebody else live out my dream. It just didn't seem possible that I was a mother, and I was actually taking my baby home! I had dreamed of having a baby for a couple of years, and I couldn't believe that my dream was finally reality. Reflecting back on this thirty-five years later still brings tears to my eyes as I recall the rush of emotion that first night when I nursed Sarah and placed her lovingly in her cradle.

Over the course of the next few weeks, Sarah and I went through sore nipples, mastitis, and frequent spurts of uncontrollable crying (I'm not sure which of us was crying harder!) I called the wonderful lactation consultant from the hospital who had given me her home phone number, multiple times. The good news is that we made it to the one month mark and never looked back!

As you bring your baby home from the hospital, there are several things you need to consider.

Where baby will sleep

Before Sarah was born I had read a book on parenting from the 1970's that emphasized the importance of not spoiling your baby. It said one very important thing to do from the beginning was to make sure your baby NEVER slept in the bed with you. It also directed mothers to let their babies cry themselves to sleep if they wouldn't go down peacefully. Oh, did I mention that Sarah was a VERY high need baby???? As you might imagine, that advice coupled with a sensitive high need baby (who became a strong-willed child) was a recipe for disaster.

I would nurse Sarah. She would fall asleep. I would lay her in her cradle. She would wake up and cry. I thought I was doing her a favor by letting her lie there and cry until she fell asleep. After 5 minutes I would go in and pat her back, then leave again. Ten minutes, then fifteen minutes later I was back again, repeating my attempts at comforting her. By the time she was 3 or 4 months there were nights when I would lie awake on my side of the wall listening to her cry on her side of the wall for over an hour. I was crying, too.

When Sarah was almost six months old, someone gave me a copy of the wonderful book by William Sears, MD, Christian Parenting and Child Care (Broadman and Holman). That book should be on every Christian mother's bookshelf. It is truly a Biblical guide to every aspect of parenting. I learned that it was actually natural and Biblical for babies to sleep in the same room, or even the same bed as their parents. I learned that you can't spoil a newborn. By meeting his needs you are teaching him trust, not spoiling him. In fact, meeting your infant's needs lays a strong foundation for later discipline. I was tremendously relieved to know that I didn't have to listen to Sarah cry another night! My husband and I agreed that the best place for her was in our bed! We all began sleeping much better!

Parents and babies sleeping in separate rooms is a relatively modern notion. Throughout the ages, and even now in many parts of the world, it has been and continues to be common practice for babies to sleep with their mothers. Certainly where your baby sleeps is a decision you must make together with your husband. If he completely objects to having the baby in your bed, then you need to respect that.

You should be aware that recently the American Academy of Pediatrics has issued a statement about where infants should sleep. They recommend "a separate but proximate sleeping environment." (Pediatrics Vol 116, No. 5, November 2005, p.1252) For additional information on this issue, see www://askdrsears,com/html/10/t102200.as

If you don't want your baby actually sleeping in your bed with you, consider having his cradle or crib in your room for at least the first six weeks of his life. It makes it much easier on you when it's time to feed him in the middle of the night. One mother explained that she would awaken her husband to get the baby out of his crib at the foot of their bed and bring him to her. Hubby would fall back asleep while she was nursing, then she would awaken him again to put the baby back in the crib. That was one loving, patient husband!

If you do choose to have your baby with you, it is best to have a firm mattress. Dr. Sears says that the best piece of furniture new parents can buy is a king size bed! Some parents worry that they will suffocate their babies if they sleep with them. As long as a mother is not under the influence of alcohol or drugs, that won't happen. Babies and mothers who sleep together share sleep cycles. Hormonal cues from the mother actually help to regulate the baby's breathing. (Mosko) You can purchase a child's bed rail to put on your side of the bed and let the baby sleep between you and the rail so that you are still snuggled next to your husband. A wonderful option for parents who want a "separate but proximate" sleeping environment is the Arm's Reach co-sleeper which actually attaches to your bed. Either way, you will enjoy your nights so much more because you won't have to get up and go to another room to nurse!

A quiet place to nurse

During the first weeks when you are getting your milk supply established and learning all about your baby, you may find that having a quiet established place to nurse is helpful. It might be a rocking chair in the nursery. It might be a big comfy chair in the living room. Or it might be propped up with pillows in your own bed. No matter where it is, there are several things that are indispensable. The first is pillows….several of them. You will want a pillow to go under the baby. You might want one under your arm if you are using a reverse cradle hold or a football hold. You may want one behind you, as well, especially if you are sitting up in bed.

Another important thing to consider if you are in a chair is the position of your feet. A special nursing footstool will put your feet at just the right angle for you to be able to nurse very comfortably. You can find nursing footstools on the internet or at any store that carries breastfeeding supplies.

Finally, it is nice to have a glass of water or juice to drink as you are nursing. Try to have a table beside your chair or bed where you can conveniently reach your drink. Nursing mothers need enough water or juice to be well hydrated. You don't have to drink milk to make milk. However, if your body is not properly hydrated, it may affect your milk supply. So when you sit down to nurse, have a drink nearby to quench your thirst. If you have an older child, asking him to bring you one is an ideal way to enlist his help and make him feel very useful.

Knowing when to nurse

One of the books I read while I was pregnant with my first child said that all infants must be placed on a strict schedule. After all, went the reasoning, parents must be in control, not babies. Unfortunately, there are still many in the Christian community who believe that scheduling is the key to Christian parenting. However, I am convinced that a far wiser way to parent from the very beginning is by learning your baby's cues. Before a baby begins to cry with hunger, he will exhibit certain behaviors to let you know it's time to eat. These include putting his hand in his mouth, rooting (when your baby is opening his mouth in response to something touching his cheek), and sucking. When you see these cues, you will know it's time to feed him. A mother who is attentive to her infant's cues may find that her baby rarely cries. He doesn't need to cry much because he has learned to trust his mother to respond to his cues.

Some babies are very sleepy during the first week or so. Knowing when to feed these babies can be a challenge. Remember the important rule of thumb that a newborn needs to nurse 8 – 12 times in a 24 hour period. Waking a baby who is in a deep sleep is almost impossible, so you need to learn the behaviors that will let you know he is in a light enough sleep to be awakened. You may see him bring his fist to his mouth or begin to suck. He may move some and seem a bit restless in his sleep. While his eyes might not completely open, the eyelids might flutter.

Watch for these signs, and when you see them, pick your newborn up and undress him. Check his diaper and change it if necessary. Usually that will awaken him! If he still seems groggy, leave him undressed with just a diaper on. Then take off your shirt and bra, and allow him to have skin-to-skin contact with you. If it is chilly, you can put a blanket over the two of you. Often, the skin to skin contact will stimulate a sleepy baby to awaken enough to nurse.

Carrying and comforting your baby

Your baby has been balled up in your womb for the last nine months. He is used to being in a tight, confined area. Therefore, he will feel more secure if he is snugly wrapped or carried in a snug carrier. Swaddling, where an infant is wrapped in a receiving blanket like a little burrito, is a wonderful way to comfort a fussy newborn. Before you leave your birthing facility, make sure a nurse shows you how to swaddle your baby properly. Even if someone doesn't teach you, it's not hard to learn how to swaddle your baby. Just follow these simple steps:

- Lay a baby blanket out flat, and fold one corner down.

- Place baby in the center of the blanket with his head on the folded down corner.

- Fold one side over the baby snugly.

- Bring the bottom up, then fold the remaining side over the baby so that he is snugly wrapped up like a little burrito.

Many mothers have found that wearing their babies in a carrier is also very comforting. A variety of carriers exist. Before Sarah was born I bought a frontpack carrier. But when I put her in it, her little head wobbled over to the side, and she just looked very uncomfortable. It didn't feel comfortable to me either. Then I found out about baby slings!

Because of their popularity and wonderful suitability for nursing, many kinds of baby slings exist. I found that a ring sling was ideal for my situation. A good sling will offer privacy while breastfeeding; it will be sized to fit the mother, and it will be versatile, lasting from birth through toddlerhood. When you put your sling on, normally the pad will rest on your shoulder. However, for a newborn, you might find it more comfortable to allow the pad to serve as a pillow. You will read more about other types of baby carriers in chapter 12.

Colic

Some babies become colicky when they are two to three weeks old. A baby with colic will cry inconsolably, usually during the evening hours. By the time they are three months old, most babies outgrow colic. Often wearing your baby in a sling during these hours and allowing him to nurse frequently will help soothe the colic. Some mothers find that giving the baby a warm bath soothes him and helps him settle down for the night. Baby's Bliss sells a product called "Gripe Water" which is a ginger-based natural remedy for colic. The moms in our practice have found it to be more effective than mylecon drops.

The classic "colic carry" usually helps relieve the discomfort. Put a dry towel in the microwave for about a minute; then lay it over your forearm. Hold baby face down with his tummy on the towel, his head in your hand, and his legs hanging down on either side. With your other hand on top of his back, gently move your arm back and forth, up and down. The movement combined with the heat and the pressure on his little belly will help make him more comfortable.

Nobody knows exactly why some babies are prone to colic while others rarely fuss at all. Sometimes if a baby is getting too much foremilk and not enough hindmilk, he may have colic-like symptoms. The first thing you should do is be sure that your baby is completely finishing the first breast before he goes to the second one. If you are still taking iron supplements, that could be causing your baby's colic. So before you try eliminating any foods, stop taking the iron supplements. Be sure to check your multi-vitamin (or pre-natal) to make sure it doesn't have iron.

If, after five days, you still don't see any difference, you can try eliminating all dairy products from your diet. Sometimes dairy products can cause an allergic reaction in some infants which will manifest in colicky behavior. Again, if dairy products are the culprit, you will notice a difference within five days. Another common allergen is soy protein. So if the colic continues, you can try eliminating soy. If you still see no improvement, you need to talk with a lactation consultant or your baby's doctor. Gastro-esophageal reflux can also produce colic-like symptoms in a newborn; this is a condition that responds well to medication.

Sleeping through the night

It is absolutely unrealistic to expect a breastfed newborn to sleep through the night. Sometimes the mother of a formula-fed baby will boast that her baby has slept through the night since the day they brought him home. That just is not what babies are designed to do! Breastmilk is especially formulated by its Maker to be readily absorbed by the baby's intestines. Therefore, within 2-3 hours after eating, he will be ready to eat again. Nevertheless, most newborns will have one period when they will sleep four or even five hours at a stretch. The trick is to help them learn that this 4 – 5 hour stretch needs to happen at night!

Many mothers complain that their infants have their days and nights mixed up. That is not an uncommon problem. Nevertheless, there is a fairly simple way to teach a baby to sleep longer at night than during the day. You simply awaken him to nurse every 2 – 2 ½ hours during the day, even when tempted to just let him sleep.

After several days of being awakened to nurse every 2 to 2 ½ hours during the day, your baby will begin to awaken by himself to nurse during the day. You will also find that he begins to have his longer stretch of sleep at night. Always be sure, though, that your baby is nursing at least 8 times in a 24 hour period during the first few weeks.

Beginning a bedtime routine

As you are helping your baby learn to have his longest stretch of sleep at night, one important component of your parenting is your bedtime routine. Figure out what time you want him to go to sleep for his four or five hour stretch. This will vary from one family to another depending on your own sleep patterns. If he goes down at 8:00, he will probably be waking up by 1:00. If he doesn't go down until 11:00, he might sleep until 4:00. As he gets older and sleeps for a longer stretch, you can vary his bedtime accordingly.

Once you have decided when bedtime is, you need to have a specific routine that you follow each night. Your baby will learn that when you follow these specific steps, it is time for him to settle into a deep sleep. One very relaxing component of the bedtime routine can be the bath. Some babies hate to be bathed at first, so this might not be relaxing to your baby if he doesn't enjoy it. Until his umbilical cord has completely dried up and fallen off, you need to sponge bathe him with warm water. Make sure you are in a warm room so that his undressed, damp body doesn't feel cold. After a couple of weeks he will be ready to be immersed in a warm bath. A baby bathtub makes it easy for you to hold onto him and help him learn to really enjoy this process. Be sure the water is warm, but not too hot, and the room temperature is warm, too. Have a soft towel ready to snuggle him as soon as he is done.

After the bath, you can dress him in his night clothes. Then go to a specific place to nurse. For the bedtime routine, it is good to choose a quiet, dimly lit place where you can nurse comfortably and without interruption. Sitting in front of the TV doesn't cut it! As you are nursing, focus on your baby. Sing to him and pray for him. Perhaps you will have a CD of lullabies that you play for him. Your Christian bookstore will have a good selection of wonderful lullabies for babies. You might even make up a song just for him. I wrote a song about the meaning of each one of my children's names. I would sing it to them every night as I nursed them to sleep. Often I would sing it during the day, too. But at night, it was part of our routine. It's amazing that even at 6 and 10 my younger two children sometimes still asked me to sing them their songs as I prayed with them before bed.

You are beginning a routine that will last for many years. Although it will change as your children grow from one stage to another, one very important element can last well into their teens: your prayers. You have the awesome privilege of bringing your baby before the throne of God Almighty. As you hold this precious infant in your arms, you can pray for his health, for his development, for his future, and most importantly, that he will come to know and love the Lord at an early age.   When you pray for and with your child each night, you are leaving him a legacy that will go with him throughout his life.

I prayed that way for Daniel from the day he was born. When he was two and a half he began asking a lot of questions about why Jesus had to die on the cross. One morning he came into the living room one morning while I was having my devotions. He knew that he wasn't supposed to interrupt "Mommy-Jesus time." But he just couldn't help himself as he told me he wanted to be sure he was going to Heaven. I told him the precious Gospel story once again, and he prayed in his own words asking Jesus to be his savior. Afterwards, he was so excited he ran in and woke up his big sister to tell her about his decision. Then he ran into the bathroom where his dad was showering to tell him. By the time Daniel was a teenager, we could see in him a sincere commitment to the Lord. The last two summers of high school he raised money to go on mission trips. In fact, our church gave him a generous gift because they could see the caliber of young man he was and his love for the Lord. As an adult he has experienced highs and lows in his faith-walk, but we know that the Father has an amazing plan for him.

Knowing that your baby is getting enough milk

Many new mothers worry that their babies might not be getting enough milk. Certainly it is very dangerous if a breastfed baby does not receive an adequate milk supply. Complicating the matter is that some babies who are actually very hungry don't cry; they are too weak to do much but just sleep. You can know for certain that your baby is getting enough milk by looking at the following indicators:

• You are nursing 8 – 12 times in a 24 hour period. When you nurse, you can see and hear your baby rhythmically sucking and swallowing.

• Your baby has at least 6 – 8 wet diapers and at least 3 - 4 bowel movements in a 24 hour period. If you are using cloth diapers, there will probably be 10 – 12 wet diapers. Your baby's urine should be clear, not yellow, and it shouldn't have a strong ammonia odor. The first few days of your baby's life, his bowel movements will be meconium which looks like black tar. Once your colostrum begins to change to milk, his stools will be yellowish and quite soft. The consistency and color has been compared to Grey Poupon Honey Dijon mustard.

• Your baby has increasing periods where he is in a quiet alert state, contentedly watching the world around him. Some very sensitive babies do not want to be put down, but will contentedly watch the world from the security of your arms. If your baby seems to sleep more and more, then you would be wise to seek medical attention.

• Your baby has regained his birth weight by the third week and continues gaining ⅓ to ½ pound per week. Most babies do lose 5 – 10% of their birth weight in the first days after birth. However, a baby who is nursing well will gain that back by the end of the second week and will keep on growing steadily.

Seeing the lactation consultant

Many hospitals provide an International Board Certified Lactation Consultant (IBCLC) to help new mothers learn how to successfully breastfeed their babies. The IBCLC designation assures you that you are getting the best possible breastfeeding support. To earn that designation, a health care worker must have received specific training in breastfeeding management and support, must have demonstrated extensive experience working with breastfeeding mothers and babies, and must have passed a rigorous board exam. IBCLCs are required to maintain their certification through on-going education and must recertify every five years. Therefore, when you have an IBCLC working with you, you can be confident that you are getting the best support possible.

In some hospitals all breastfeeding mothers receive a routine visit from the lactation consultant. Other hospitals have many postpartum nurses who are knowledgeable about breastfeeding, and the lactation consultant is only called in when there is a challenging situation. Either way, you should have someone from the hospital staff who is able to help you and your baby get off to a good start. If you don't feel like you are getting the help and support you need, ask to see a nurse who specializes in lactation. If you need help locating a lactation consultant, you may search for one at the following site sponsored by the International Lactation Consultant Association: http://gotwww.net/ilca/ or you may look at the International Board of Lactation Consultant Examiners' registry of US lactation consultants located at http://www.iblce.org/US%20registry.htm

Occasionally a mother will express shock at the cost of a consultation. Although some insurance companies do reimburse for a visit to a lactation consultant, many still do not. However, I encourage mothers to look at the cost as an investment in their baby's health. Instead of giving up breastfeeding and switching to a costly formula, a mother who sees a lactation consultant will usually be able to solve her nursing problems and enjoy a successful breastfeeding relationship. The costs, both economically and physically, of using a breastmilk substitute are infinitely higher than the cost of seeing a good lactation consultant.

When Shauna asked if I would come for a home visit to help her with 10 day old Garrett, I wasn't prepared for what I found when I arrived. Garrett was obviously dehydrated and in real danger. When I asked Shauna about his wet diapers and stools, she said that he was only having a couple of wet diapers a day....and they smelled funny. She then told me that he just wouldn't awaken to nurse. She had tried everything! I didn't even let her try to nurse him at that point. I told her she needed to get him to his pediatrician as soon as possible. She was frightened, but took him right away to the doctor who put him into the hospital immediately for hydration.

As Shauna and I discussed what had happened, she told me she had been reading a Christian parenting book that said parents should schedule their baby's feedings every three to four hours. She had been nursing Garrett every four hours. However, they had several problems. First of all, he wasn't latching on correctly. Secondly, because he wasn't nursing frequently, or sucking correctly when he did nurse, her body wasn't producing very much milk. She hadn't realized he was starving and dehydrating. She just thought he was a really good baby who didn't fuss very much at all. Garrett recovered well, but Shauna was too shaken to continue nursing. Although I tried to help her, she just didn't want to try anymore.

You can avoid a crisis like Shauna's by following the guidelines given in this chapter. If, at any point, you feel that something just isn't right, call your lactation consultant. I have gotten calls in the middle of the night from distraught mothers. That just goes with the job! If you can wait until morning, please do, but by all means get help if you need it! God designed you to breastfeed, to enjoy, and to marvel at your precious baby. Don't let anything keep you from doing just that!

Chapter 4:

Giggles and Smiles –
Feeding Your 1- 6 Month Old

"I gave you milk to drink, not solid food; for you were not yet able to receive it."
– I Corinthians 3:2a

As I visited with month old baby Henry at his house, his mom asked me, "Is that a sweet little smile? Or is it just gas?" By the time your baby is a month old, it will certainly seem that he really is smiling at you. He will spend more and more time in a quiet alert state where he observes his surroundings. He is able to lift his head a little bit and maybe even turn it from side to side. His little eyes may have begun to follow a rattle as you move it from side to side.

By the time your baby is six weeks old, he is no longer really a newborn. You may begin to notice some changes in his feeding patterns as well as in his diapers. It will help if you know what to expect. Sometimes mothers actually stop breastfeeding at this point because they don't understand what is happening.

Growth Spurts

MaryAnn called me in a panic. She was sure that she had lost her milk supply because six week old Brandon was always hungry. She was in tears as she told me that she had nursed him from 10 until 10:40 in the morning, and by 11:30 he wanted to be nursed again. She said that she really wanted to nurse him, but hated to see him so hungry.

When I told MaryAnn about growth spurts and helped her understand how to work with Brandon during this time, she was extremely relieved. Mary Ann set aside the next two days and just stayed in bed with Brandon most of the day, resting and nursing as often as he wanted. He continued nursing frequently for about five days, then went back to nursing about every 2 ½ - 3 hours during the day and once around 2:00 in the morning.

A growth spurt occurs when your baby enters a phase where he needs more breastmilk. Typical times for growth spurts are around 3 weeks, 6 weeks, 3 months, and from 4 - 6 months. However, a growth spurt can occur earlier or later. Anytime your baby seems to nurse ALL THE TIME, he is probably in a growth spurt. Usually they last 2-3 days; however, a growth spurt can last up to a week.

When you realize that your baby is nursing more frequently you may be tempted to supplement. Or you may have a well meaning relative say, "Give that baby some formula....can't you see he's starving?" DON'T!!! Remember that your body makes milk on a demand/supply basis. The more your baby nurses, the more milk your body will make. If you meet his additional needs with a supplement, you are actually circumventing the process that God so wisely set in place for you to provide for all your baby's needs.

The wisest thing you can do during a growth spurt is set everything else aside and focus on your baby for two or three days. If you have other children, this is a great time to take advantage of those offers that your friends have made to help. Or maybe you can send them to Grandma's house for a few days. You need to try to do what MaryAnn did. Rest, eat properly and drink water or juice whenever you are thirsty, and nurse as often as you need to. It's actually kind of nice just to baby yourself and your infant; enjoy long naps together. You might even be able to read a good book as you and baby just stay in bed and nurse. This is also a great time for your husband to minister to you and your baby as he takes care of you.

Another way to cope with growth spurts is to wear your baby in a sling so that he has access to your breast whenever he needs it. If you absolutely can't take off and go to bed, this is the next best option. Mothers who are busy with other children may find that the sling is a life-saver during growth spurts. However, if you can take at least one nap a day with your baby during his growth spurt, you will both handle things much better (especially you!)

Depending on their ages, your older children can play a quiet game, read quietly, watch a special video or take naps themselves. If you have a big enough bed, you might even be able to get kids who don't nap anymore to lie down with you and baby to take a nap. You might be surprised at how much your older children enjoy being a part of this special bond that you and your new baby are forging. It is important to note here that an older child should never be next to the baby; instead have the older child on the other side of you.

Cluster nursing

Some babies "cluster" nurse. They will eat every thirty or forty-five minutes for several hours, and then sleep for several hours at a time. This isn't necessarily a growth spurt. This may simply be your baby's pattern. Both of my girls cluster nursed in the evening. From about 6:30 until about 10:00 it seemed like all we did was nurse. I learned to put my daughter in the sling and give her constant access to the breast during those hours.

Then around 9:00 we would begin a bedtime routine. I would give her a warm bath and put on her pajamas. Then we would nurse in the rocking chair while I sang to her and prayed for her. My third child, Anna Joy, learned quickly that this was bedtime. (See Bedtime routines in chapter 3).

Changing Patterns

Your growing baby will experience some changes in both feeding and stooling patterns. After he finishes a growth spurt, he may settle back into his previous nursing routine, or he might even nurse less frequently. Sometimes around three months of age, babies begin to space out their feedings. Instead of needing to nurse every 2 – 2 ½ hours, they may have periods in the day where they go 3 or 3 ½ hours between feeds. Remember, though, your exclusively breastfed baby should still nurse 7 or 8 times in a 24 hour period.

Some babies become very adept at removing mom's milk quickly. So they aren't interested in a 20 – 30 minute nursing session. Carla stopped me at church one morning and asked me if it was okay that Becky only nursed 10 minutes at a time. She was feeding every 3 hours during the day, and sleeping 7 hours at night. She did nurse for 20 minutes before bed. Four month old Becky was obviously gaining weight quite well and was very healthy. Carla's fatty milk clearly let-down early in the feed, and Becky was getting plenty of it early on, so she was satisfied.

Stooling patterns

Another pattern that might change is your baby's stooling pattern. Typically a newborn may have a dirty diaper almost every time he eats. However, as his intestines are better able to use all of the breastmilk, he may have less frequent bowel movements. It is not unusual for a breastfed infant between 2 and 6 months to have only one dirty diaper every 4 or 5 days. Some babies can go as long as a week. On the other hand, it is also completely normal for a breastfed baby of that age to have one or two dirty diapers a day.

You know your baby better than anybody else. As long as he doesn't seem like he is experiencing discomfort, he is probably fine. While he is exclusively breastfed, you won't normally need to worry about variations in the number of dirty diapers.

Some mothers do worry about the variations in color of the stool. If your baby's bowel movements are very mucousy or bloody, it could be that he is experiencing an allergic reaction to something in your diet. See the section on food allergies in chapter 7 for more information about this. A mucousy diaper can also be caused by teething. Often a baby who is teething will also have a bright red diaper rash.

If your baby's stool is very green in color, it could be due to his not getting enough fatty milk toward the end of a feed. The solution is to let him nurse longer on one breast. Make sure that he gets as much hindmilk as he can. In fact, let him control how long he feeds on the first breast. You can use breast massage to keep the milk flowing if he is a very lazy or sleepy nurser.

Any time that you have a concern, call your lactation consultant. She will be able to ask you specific questions to evaluate your specific situation. If you need to see your pediatrician, she will be quick to encourage you to do that. Most lactation consultants don't mind answering ongoing questions for moms whom they have seen. However, if a lactation consultant hasn't ever seen you and your baby, you do need to make an appointment to see her so she can perform a complete evaluation.

Teething

Sometime during this period your baby will begin teething. Some babies begin as early as six weeks, and others don't start until three, four or even six months. When your baby is teething, you will notice that he seems to drool all the time. In fact, you might want to let him wear a drool bib so that he won't ruin the lovely little outfit Aunt Bertha bought him! He will want to have something in his mouth all the time. It might be his hand, his clothes, or a toy you provide for him.

His little gums are very tender, and he might be a lot fussier than usual during this time. As mentioned above, his little bottom might be sore, too, from the rash caused by the extra mucous he is producing and swallowing. Some babies want to nurse more when they are teething. Often, they are nursing for comfort. That is fine; in fact, it has been demonstrated that there are substances in breastmilk that do help to soothe a baby.

Sometimes, however, a teething baby may try to bite while he is nursing. Do NOT allow him to do this. The very first time he bites, remove him by breaking the suction. Tell him lovingly, but firmly, that he may not bite while he is nursing, and put your breast away. If he is biting, he isn't really hungry. Find another way to soothe and comfort him. Then when he is actually hungry (watch for his cues) feed him like normal. You don't ever want to allow your baby to bite or tug on your nipple because this can cause real damage to your nipples. This correcting of your baby when he bites you is actually part of your baby's earliest discipline: you are lovingly teaching your baby how to behave. There are several things you can do to help ease the discomfort that your teething baby is experiencing.

• Use a teething ring that you can refrigerate. Make sure you choose one that is textured.

• Moisten infant washcloths with boiled or purified water. Then place them in zip-lock bags in the freezer. Pull one out before feeding time and let baby chew on it. The rough texture on the washcloth will feel good on his gums, and the cold will numb them.

• If he is running a fever or has cold-like symptoms, ask his doctor what medication you should give him. Many doctors recommend infant Tylenol drops to help relieve the discomfort of teething.

• There are also homeopathic remedies available for teething. Check with your local pharmacy or natural food store.

Interacting with your baby

As you begin to see more of your baby's personality developing, you will find real joy in making him smile, giggle and laugh. The more you play and interact with him, the more joy he will bring you. Don't make the mistake of assuming that he is too young to play. Your 6-week old baby will enjoy watching the changes in your face as you smile and talk to him. Soon he will begin imitating your facial expressions!

You are the most important person in your baby's world. When he hears your voice, he will turn towards you. As he grows, he will reach for you when you are close. You may find that your three or four month old baby doesn't want to be left with anybody else. Some babies are extremely attached to their mothers. Research has shown that early attachment often leads to greater independence later on. Daniel, my second child, never minded going into the church nursery. In fact, he was all smiles when we left him. Anna Joy, our third, hated to be left in a nursery. So I just kept her with me in the sling. She didn't cry; in fact, she pretty much learned to sleep through church. Be sensitive to what your baby needs, and don't allow others to tell you what is best for your baby!

During these first six months your baby will learn many new things. He will learn to roll over. One morning you might place him on his blanket in the middle of the floor, leave the room for a moment and come back to find that he has rolled across the room. He will also enjoy reaching for brightly colored toys and exploring them by putting them in his mouth. He will love it when you play peek-a-boo with him.

Another important interaction for you to begin during this time period is reading to your baby. Choose books that he can put in his mouth. The brightly colored pictures will grab his attention. Check at your Christian bookstore for books in the Baby Bible series by Robin Currie. It's never too early to begin sharing the treasures of God's Word with your baby. As you nurture your infant at your breast, singing to him and telling him about Jesus' love, you are building a firm foundation to carry him forward into childhood, the turbulent teenage years, and finally adulthood.

Chapter 5:

Upwardly Mobile –
Feeding Your Older Baby

*"For thus says the LORD, "Behold, I extend peace
to her like a river, And the glory of the nations like
an overflowing stream; And you will be nursed, you
will be carried on the hip and fondled on the knees."*

– Isaiah 66:12

Daniel was about 5 ½ months old when we went to Florida to visit my in-laws. We went to eat at a Wendy's that had a salad bar. I loaded my plate with all kinds of delicious fruits and veggies. Daniel was still exclusively breastfed at this point, but he sat in his high chair watching my every move and even trying to reach for my food. My father-in-law said, "Give that boy some watermelon; he's starving!" I knew he wasn't starving because he had just nursed before we left home, and I really hadn't planned to start solids for another couple of weeks. Nevertheless, I thought I'd see what happened if I gave him a very small piece of the watermelon. He was so excited when he got it between his thumb and finger and into his mouth. And boy did he like that watermelon!

Your baby is no longer a tiny infant. He is probably exhibiting signs that he is ready to begin solid food now. You will have many questions in these next few months, such as "How do I begin feeding solids?" "What do I do if he doesn't want to nurse?" and "How long should I keep nursing my baby?" You've come to the right place to find the answers!

Solid foods

Up until this point your baby has only had milk to drink. But around the sixth month of his life, some developmental milestones will occur that indicate his readiness for solid food. God designed your baby in such a way that your milk provides all the nutrients his growing body and developing brain needed during those first six months. Now, however, he is physically, psychologically and emotionally ready to begin eating solid food.

Signs that your baby is ready

Some babies exhibit these signs earlier and some later. Instead of looking for a magic age (6 months from the day he was born), watch for these signs. Just as you learned to nurse him on cue, you will begin feeding him solids when he lets you know he is ready. Here are the indicators that your baby is ready to begin solid foods.

• He shows interest in the foods you are eating. At mealtime, his eyes follow every bite you eat from your plate to your mouth.

• He has lost the tongue thrust reflex. When you put food into his mouth, he doesn't push it back at you with his tongue. If he is truly ready for solids, he will accept them eagerly.

• He is able to sit up by himself. If he can sit up in a high-chair, he is probably ready to begin eating. When Sarah turned four months old, my pediatrician said she could start on cereal. Because she couldn't sit up by herself at that age, I would tie a long baby blanket around her waist to hold her in the chair. She certainly wasn't ready for solids; in fact, she hated being tied into her high chair and fed. I had never read about readiness for solids, and I just didn't know any better!

• He has developed the pincer grasp where he can pick up things using his thumb and forefinger. This is extremely useful when he is sitting in his high chair while you are eating. Give him a few Cheerios at a time, and he will be a happy camper.

• He may have begun getting teeth.

How to begin feeding solids

You must remember that your baby's primary nourishment throughout the first year of his life will come from your milk. Therefore, it is important to nurse him first, before you offer him solid food. If you ask five different pediatricians, nutritionists and lactation consultants what you should feed first, you might get five different answers. Many pediatricians recommend rice cereal first because they have patients who are only four months old (or younger) beginning on solids. If you wait until your baby is truly ready for solids, you won't even need to worry about feeding him traditional store-bought baby cereals and jars of baby food. In fact, the healthiest foods for your baby are the foods that your family eats on a regular basis!

You might begin with a hot cereal (cooled, of course) like grits, oatmeal or brown rice. Or you might prefer to start with a vegetable like potatoes or carrots. Some mothers find that bananas or avocados make a wonderful first food because they are so easy to mash. Whatever food you choose, make sure that you breastfeed first and begin by feeding just a teaspoon or two of food.

After introducing a new food, wait at least two or three days before introducing another new food. This will give you time to make sure that he isn't exhibiting any kind of allergic reaction to the new food. Symptoms of a food allergy can include redness or a rash in the diaper area, a runny nose, a skin rash, or excessive fussiness. If he seems to have any of these symptoms, stop giving him the food and see if they clear up within 3 or 4 days. If they do, then you will know not to feed him that particular food for a while. You can try again in several months to see how he tolerates it then.

A small food processor or handheld baby food grinder is a

wonderful gadget to have when you begin feeding your baby solid foods. You can just use food from your family's meal, add a little water or breastmilk, and grind it to a consistency that will be ideal for your baby. Once your baby has tried peas, carrots, and potatoes, for example, you might take a little bit of the beef stew you fixed for dinner, grind it up, and give it to him for dinner (after you nurse him, of course.) If he has several teeth, you might find that he would prefer you to put small pieces of the carrot, potato, peas and beef on his highchair tray and let him feed himself.

The beauty of waiting until he is truly ready for solids is that he will delight in feeding himself at the same time as you are eating. Of course, you can't expect him to have great coordination with the spoon at first; in fact, fingers work just fine for a baby learning to feed himself. One of the greatest recent inventions I have seen is a big vinyl "highchair mat" that goes under the highchair and extends out about a foot all the way around. It will cut your post-meal clean-up time significantly!

While I don't recommend watermelon as a first food generally speaking, the opening story does illustrate the point that when a baby is ready to eat, he will do so and LOVE it! Even though Daniel kept on nursing for 2 ½ more years, once he got that first bite of watermelon, he wanted to eat everything in sight!

Whereas some babies are eager for solid food before they are six months old, other babies may not be interested at all in eating anything but breastmilk. Yolanda came to me very concerned that her extremely healthy 8 month old baby, Gabrielle, wasn't showing much interest in solid food. Her pediatrician had checked Gabrielle's iron level and found it to be normal. As I explored the health history, I found that both Yolanda and her husband had fairly severe food allergies. Gabrielle was still nursing about 5 times during the day; at night she slept with Yolanda and nursed off and on especially toward the morning hours. Her weight gain was excellent; her development was actually ahead of schedule in some areas, and she was a very happy baby. The pediatrician wasn't overly concerned, and I encouraged Yolanda to continue offering solids, especially finger foods that Gabrielle could eat by herself, but not to worry.

Interestingly enough, despite the family history of food allergies, Gabrielle didn't have much problem. It seemed as if God had designed her little system to know that it just couldn't handle solid food very early. By the time Gabrielle was a year old, she was eating more solids, but still loved to nurse. If you have a baby who, like Gabrielle, isn't interested in solids, just make healthy finger foods available, and sooner or later, he will eat!

Introducing a Cup

A baby who is able to sit in a highchair and has the fine motor skills necessary to feed himself is certainly able to begin drinking from a cup. If you have expressed breastmilk, you can feed him that with his meal. Many moms used to give their babies diluted fruit juice. But the AAP recommends that babies not receive any juice at all during the first year of life. A much better choice would be to offer him water in the cup. Be sure to choose a cup that has a spill-proof lid or you will have liquid everywhere. Patience is important, but if he keeps throwing the cup off his highchair tray, then put it aside and offer it to him a few minutes later. Whatever you do, don't let mealtime become a battleground. It should be a fun time for both you and your baby.

Continue Breastfeeding

The American Academy of Pediatrics has the following statement in its policy statement on breastfeeding: "The AAP supports continued breastfeeding, along with appropriate complementary foods introduced at about 6 months, as long as mutually desired by mother and child for 2 years or beyond." (AAP Policy Statement, Pediatrics Vol.150 No.1 July 2022) The medical and scientific communities recognize the important role that breastmilk continues to play in both protecting and nourishing the older infant. They agree that no baby should be given cow's milk before one year of age because there appears to be a link between early introduction of cow's milk protein and juvenile diabetes.

Nursing your 6 – 12 month old

Even though your baby has begun eating solid foods, your breastmilk will still meet about 75% of his nutritional needs throughout the first year of his life. During these months, you will want to make sure that you nurse your baby before he eats. You don't want him to fill up on other foods and then not take enough of your milk. Although your baby may only nurse five or six times in a 24 hour period, he will have become very adept at getting what he needs pretty quickly. You may find that he nurses for ten or fifteen minutes and is completely full.

As his diet changes to include more solids, you will also notice some changes in his diapers. His bowel movements will no longer have the smooth yellow mustard-like consistency that they had when he was exclusively breastfed. He may actually have less frequent bowel movements, or he may have one every day. If he has four or five stools a day at this age, he might have diarrhea. Eliminate whatever new food you just began and watch him closely. If it continues, call your pediatrician.

Distractibility

As your baby grows, he will be increasingly curious about the world around him. Some babies are so intrigued by their surroundings that they can barely be still long enough to nurse. If you find that your baby nurses for a few minutes, then stops and looks around before going back to eat for a few more minutes, you may have an inquisitive little guy who just wants to expand his horizons. It's up to you to design a nursing environment that will help your baby nurse without distractions. Have a quiet place to nurse where he won't be sidetracked by noise from the TV, radio or other children. Dim the lights so that he isn't tempted to look around. Most importantly, focus your complete attention on him while he nurses; you might find that singing the songs you sang to him when he was a newborn will help him to settle down and nurse.

Nursing Strikes

It isn't unusual for a 9 or 10 month old baby to suddenly refuse the breast. His mother may be startled, and think he has weaned himself. That isn't the case at all; he is just going through a nursing strike. Sometimes all the exciting things that are happening in his life distract him so much that he just doesn't have time to nurse, or maybe he doesn't want to be bothered with nursing when there are other things he could be doing. If you aren't ready to wean yet, then be sure you pump to maintain your supply. Try nursing at night when he is really sleepy. Make sure you're in a dark, quiet place so he won't be distracted. Usually a nursing strike lasts less than a week, so be patient, and soon he'll be nursing again like normal

Nursing your toddler

When Sarah had her first birthday I realized that I just wasn't ready to stop nursing, and neither was she. Many mothers who have planned to nurse for a year find themselves in a similar situation. In the next chapter we will talk about how and when to wean your baby. Here, though, I want to address mothers who have decided to keep on nursing into toddlerhood. As long as your baby is receiving your milk, he continues to receive valuable antibodies and ongoing protection from illness. When he does get sick, he will probably recover more quickly thanks to the properties of your breastmilk he is receiving.

Unfortunately, we live in a society that has perverted and sexualized everything. You may have people around you who are appalled that you are still nursing a child who can walk and talk. It is appropriate to use discretion in when and where you nurse your older child. As a Christian, you do want to avoid giving any cause for offense. Nevertheless, remember that your decision to keep on nursing your child certainly has a Biblical basis. You are doing what you feel is best and wisest for your child.

Setting Boundaries

When he was an infant, you nursed your baby according to his cues, making sure that he ate at least every 3 hours during the day. Instead of creating a rigid schedule, you nursed him when he needed to be nursed. As he enters toddlerhood, however, you no longer need to nurse every time he wants to. It is appropriate to begin setting some limits now.

Throughout his life you will be giving him parameters to help him know what behavior is expected. Some mothers make the mistake of thinking that "feeding on cue" applies to breastfeeding children of all ages. It doesn't. There are sound medical reasons for you to feed your infant on cue. However, your toddler is now eating a wide variety of foods. Although he still receives some of his nutrition from your milk, it is no longer his primary source of nutrition. It is time for him to learn that there is a time and a place for nursing. By teaching your toddler when and where he may nurse, you are providing loving guidelines that let him know you are in charge. It is certainly never too early to begin establishing that fact in his mind.

Mothers who allow their toddlers to rule the roost in the area of breastfeeding have abrogated their authority. In fact, this is the reason that nursing toddlers are often viewed as little tyrants. If you are allowing him to control you in this area, chances are you are allowing him to control you in other areas as well. Your child wants and needs loving limits. He may act like he wants to be in control, but he really NEEDS for you to be in charge. A mother who provides routine and a sense of stability for her toddler will find that he grows into a happy, well-adjusted preschooler.

Many mothers teach their children a special word to use when they want to nurse. Words like num-num, yummies, milky, or mama are commonly used code words for nursing. You might have another word that you and your baby use. When he begins asking to nurse at an inconvenient time, you can distract him or help him understand that he will get to nurse later, but not right now. If he does pitch a fit, DO NOT give in and nurse. He might really be hungry or thirsty, so offer him a drink or a nutritious snack. However, part of his healthy development involves learning the principle of delayed gratification. Even a one-year old can begin to understand that, although he can't nurse right now, he may have a drink or a snack, and he will be able to nurse when you are alone together later on.

The wonderful foundation for discipline that you are laying now for your nursing toddler will help him throughout his life. The day will come when he no longer needs to nurse. But in the years to come he will need to respect you and do what you tell him to do. By nursing your baby through the first year of his life and perhaps into toddlerhood, you have laid the foundation for a life-long relationship of trust.

Chapter 6:

A Season for Everything –
Knowing When to Wean

"There is an appointed time for everything. And there is a time for every event under heaven."
– Ecclesiastes 3:1

Sarah and Abraham were delighted with their son, Isaac. He was growing and developing into the most amazing little boy. The incredible joy that he had brought into their lives was beyond anything they had ever imagined. Now Isaac was nearing the age when he would pass from babyhood into childhood. His father chose to celebrate this special occasion with a feast prepared in his honor. We read about this in Genesis 21.

You may not want to nurse your child until he is ready for a weaning feast; in fact, you may be ready for him to wean when he is a year old. On the other hand, you may find that you both still enjoy the breastfeeding relationship and aren't ready to stop when he reaches his first birthday. Readiness of both the mother and the child for weaning is the most important factor in making a decision about when to wean.

There is no specific age at which a child should wean. The American Academy of Pediatrics recommends breastfeeding through the second year of life and for as long thereafter as both mother and child want to nurse. The World Health Organization recommends breastfeeding for at least two years. For mothers in many developing countries, continued breastfeeding is a vitally important factor in providing their toddlers with optimal nutrition.

Two basic kinds of weaning exist: mother-led and child-led. Sometimes both mother and baby arrive simultaneously at the point where they are ready to move beyond the nursing relationship. That is a best-case scenario.

MOTHER-LED WEANING

When John Carl was two we were on home ministry assignment visiting churches throughout the South to raise support for our return to Peru. He still nursed at night, and we both found that in the midst of our hectic travel schedule our nursing relationship provided him a sense of security and stability. However, while we were visiting a church in Atlanta, I began having excruciating pain in my abdomen. After spending a couple of hours doubled over in a hospital waiting room, we finally discovered that I had appendicitis. Several hours later I was in surgery where the doctor was able to remove my appendix shortly before it would have burst. My recovery was complicated by pneumonia, so I ended up spending five days in the hospital.

I remember feeling so sad because I knew that this was the end of our nursing relationship. John was my last child; I knew we wouldn't have any more. And while it is certainly possible to maintain a milk supply during a hospital stay, I also realized that he was at an age and a developmental point where he was ready to wean. My family had to leave Atlanta while I was still in the hospital. It was heartbreaking kissing him good-bye and telling him he couldn't nurse. Yet when I finally did get back home, he didn't even ask to nurse. He was a big boy now and didn't need to nurse anymore. That was okay with me, because I knew that we had graduated to a new stage in our relationship.

Most mother-led weaning isn't nearly as gut-wrenching as my experience with John Carl was. Some mothers wean because they are returning to work. Others may wean because they are ready to have their body back to themselves. Some moms feel so "touched-out" that they see weaning as the only way to regain a sense of normalcy. Occasionally, a mother may have to wean because of medical reasons; nevertheless, there are relatively few medical conditions that are truly incompatible with breastfeeding.

Another reason that some mothers give for weaning is pressure from family members or friends. I hate to see mothers wean for that reason. Your relationship with your baby is between the two of you and doesn't include your mother-in-law, your sister, or your friend down the street. If pressure from others is driving your decision to wean, please spend some time carefully thinking and praying through this decision. Be sure you are weaning because you are ready to, not simply because you want to please somebody else.

Mother-led weaning is easier if a child is younger than about 15 months or older than about 2 ½. From the time he is about a year and a half old until he is around two and half, it will be more difficult for him to give up a behavior that is so deeply engrained in him. However, around 2 ½, your child's reasoning ability will have developed to the point where he can begin to understand and accept a gradual weaning.

Gradual is the key word when talking about mother-led weaning. First you might begin to nurse less frequently. Begin to lovingly say "Later" occasionally when he wants to nurse; you might also begin to shorten the time he nurses. Substitute a healthy snack or a fun activity for nursing. If he throws a tantrum, you must be consistent. Never give in to a tantrum.

The last feed to go will probably be the one at bedtime. A couple of weeks before you plan to completely wean, you might let him know that you aren't always going to nurse him until he is completely asleep. A night or two later, before nursing, you might tell him you're only going to nurse for a little while (maybe 10 minutes.) Ask him to help you out by being a big boy and falling the rest of the way asleep by himself. Nurse him until he is drowsy, then gently remove him and snuggle him. You might wait to pray with him until after you finish feeding him.

Some mothers follow Abraham's example and have a special weaning celebration. The beauty of this plan is that your child has plenty of time to adjust to the idea of weaning, and he will see it as a right of passage. A child who is three or older will respond well to this approach. Daniel and Anna Joy both had weaning parties on their birthdays. After their parties, they never asked to nurse again because they knew that they were too big for that and saw nursing as something that was for babies.

Weaning a baby younger than a year

Mothers who feel that they need to wean a baby who is younger than a year can take advantage of some of the developmental changes that he is experiencing. For example, a baby who is easily distracted might readily give up the breast to take a cup so he can keep on exploring. Some babies go on a "nursing strike" between 9 and 12 months of age. A mother who wants to wean can take advantage of the baby's temporary desire not to nurse. However, you must be careful to pump enough so that you don't get engorged. (Read more about Nusing Strikes in Chapter 5.)

Reducing your supply gradually is important if your baby is still nursing frequently. Drop one feeding and substitute a bottle or cup of formula. Wait for three or four days, then drop another feeding. Give your body time to adjust each time you drop a feeding, and your milk supply will naturally diminish.

Dealing with discomfort

Mothers who wean gradually usually do not have much problem with pain or discomfort. However, in the case of an abrupt weaning, severe engorgement can occur. If you do experience discomfort, you can use cold green cabbage leaf compresses to alleviate the pain and reduce your milk supply. Soak the leaves in cold water, then use a rolling pin to crush them. Crushing them releases the enzyme which helps reduce the fullness in your breasts. Fit them around your entire breast and change them when they begin to wilt. Although no solid medical evidence exists that cabbage leaves reduce the milk supply, many mothers do find that their milk dries up and they are much more comfortable within a week when they use the leaves. Taking sage (capsules or extract) also helps reduce the milk supply.

In the past, mothers were told to firmly bind their breasts if they wanted to make their milk dry up. Do NOT follow this advice. Not only is it painful, it can also lead to a variety of complications. If you are extremely uncomfortable, you may find that expressing just a little bit of milk will bring some relief. However, you must be very careful not to express too much. Remember the request and supply principle: if you pump until your breast is empty, you will continue to make more milk.

CHILD-LED WEANING

It is very rare for a baby to wean himself before he is a year old. In fact, most of the time they are over two before they wean themselves. However, sometimes a baby will go on a "nursing strike" where he doesn't want to nurse. Usually if a mother maintains her milk supply by pumping, her baby will go back to happily nursing within a week or so.

As a baby grows and develops into a toddler and then a preschooler, he will experience many new things. Children who nurse past infancy often find that the breastfeeding relationship offers comfort in the midst of new experiences. Yet many times they do arrive at the point by themselves where they are ready to move beyond nursing. It usually happens gradually and sometimes a mother might not even realize when her child has nursed for the last time.

Brenda had loved nursing Cody when he was an infant. As he

grew into toddlerhood, she decided that she would let him wean himself. When he was about two and a half he was down to nursing only at bedtime. If Brenda's husband put Cody to bed, he didn't even ask to nurse. About three months before his third birthday, he was only nursing once or twice a week. He just stopped asking to nurse, and Brenda felt satisfied that he had come to a point all by himself where he was ready to move on. Both Brenda and Cody had enjoyed their breastfeeding relationship, and it had come to a natural end.

Relactation

When a baby weans before his mother is ready for him to, he can go back to nursing. Relactation requires a real effort on the mother's part; however, it is very rewarding when a mother who thought that she couldn't nurse anymore is able to once again supply her baby's nutritional needs. Mothers who get off to a slow start with breastfeeding can also use a Supplemental Nursing System (SNS) or another similar device called a Lact-Aid to increase their milk supply.

Marisol called me when her daughter Gaby was 2 months old. Like many Peruvian mothers, she believed that she just couldn't make enough milk for Gaby, so she had started giving her formula. However, Gaby had allergic reactions to both milk-based and soy-based formula. A second pediatrician she consulted told her that her baby really needed breastmilk. However, Marisol's milk supply had nearly dried up.

I showed Marisol how to use a SNS, allowing her baby to receive a hypoallergenic supplement at the breast as she nursed. It wasn't easy: Marisol had to nurse Gaby with the SNS in place nine or ten times in 24 hours. However, within a week or so she began to notice that her supply was increasing. By the end of three weeks she was able to exclusively breastfeed Gaby without the SNS.

Even adoptive mothers can use one of these devices to induce lactation and supply part or all of their baby's nutritional needs. Some adoptive mothers have actually expressed a preference for the LactAid system because of its unique bag design which utilizes negative pressure to teach an infant to breastfeed. For more information on the SNS go to www.medela.com; to learn more about the LactAid go to www.LactAid.com

Untimely Weaning

Anytime a precious relationship changes, grief may result. The mother-infant relationship has turned a corner. This is actually the first of many changes a mother will experience as she and her child grow together. Parenting involves many good-byes. Although you may have said "good-bye" to breastfeeding, you certainly haven't said "good-bye" to the nurturing relationship you have worked so hard to cultivate with your child.

What is untimely weaning? It is the cessation of breastfeeding that occurs before mother and/or baby are prepared for it. It could occur shortly after birth, or it could occur when the baby is well into toddlerhood. Sometimes a medical condition or other circumstances result in a baby's weaning before his mother is ready. Such untimely weaning is often a deeply felt loss leaving an ache in a mother's heart. As a mother remembers the sweet suckling of her baby at her breast, tears may fill her eyes. It is particularly painful when a mother feels that this may be her last child.

Adding to her anguish may be a sense of guilt. A mother may think, "If I had just tried harder, he would still be nursing." Do not allow yourself to think this way. It is time to put the past behind you and focus your energy on being the mother that God wants you to be to your baby now! You need to remember that breastfeeding is NOT what makes you a good mother.

Getting beyond today's grief

How can you put this sorrow you feel behind you and press on in your mothering? Psychologists have long recognized the value of writing as a tool for coping with grief. Write a letter to your baby telling him how you felt when he nursed. Explain why you decided to breastfeed him in the first place. Describe your feelings now that he is no longer nursing. As you write, allow the cleansing tears to flow.

You might want to put the letter in your child's baby book. Or you might choose to save it until he has a baby of his own someday. If you have a daughter, she might appreciate the encouragement the letter will provide some day when she faces the weaning of her own baby.

Another useful tool for dealing with grief is talking about it with an empathetic listener. Find someone who will listen non-judgmentally. A lactation consultant, La Leche League leader or peer breastfeeding counselor would provide a good listening ear. Speak honestly about the reasons involved in your baby's weaning and the conflicting emotions you have.

Looking forward to tomorrow's parenting

After you have allowed yourself time to grieve, you need to look forward. If you allow your regrets over weaning to control your thinking, you will be unable to give your baby what he needs right now. Recognize what it is that truly makes you an outstanding mother and focus on that, not on the loss of your breastfeeding relationship. The following three factors will truly make you the mother your baby needs:

- Your trust-based relationship with your child.

- Your fervent prayers for your child.

- Your unconditional love for your child.

In Chapter 13 there is an in-depth discussion of each of these. However, as you deal with your sorrow over weaning, remember that your baby needs you to be there for him right now. He needs a mommy whom he can trust, who is praying for him daily, and who is committed to loving him no matter what!

Chapter 7:

Overcoming Bumps Along the Way –
Problems and How to Resolve Them

*"I can do all things through Christ
who strengthens me."*

– Philippians 4:13

Lisa first called me when Joel was six days old. She was concerned because he was so sleepy that he wouldn't stay awake to nurse more than about three minutes. Consequently her breasts were very engorged. When I first saw Joel, I was startled. He was exhibiting classic signs of dehydration. Lisa told me that he had only had 2 wet diapers the previous day. I told her to call her pediatrician immediately and get Joel to the hospital where he was admitted for dehydration and failure to thrive.

Remember the old saying, "Practice makes perfect"? While it may not make for perfect breastfeeding, practice certainly does help, as long as you're practicing correctly! Many of the most common problems that women encounter while they are nursing are simply the result of incorrect breastfeeding management. Therefore, a chapter on breastfeeding problems needs to begin by reiterating what correct breastfeeding looks like in the first several months

- The baby is nursing between 8 and 12 times in 24 hours
- The baby is latched on well with at least 1 ½ - 2 inches of nipple and areola in his mouth.
- You hear rhythmic sucking and swallowing.
- By day 5 the baby has at least 6 wet diapers a day and at least 3 - 4 stools.
- The baby is gaining between 5 and 8 ounces a week.
- The mother is not experiencing any nipple pain or discomfort.

If even one of these factors isn't in place, then you are at risk for significant breastfeeding problems. In fact, if your baby doesn't have sufficient wet diapers, he could actually be in danger. As soon as you realize that there might be a problem, you need to get in touch with a lactation consultant. Situations like Lisa's can be avoided if you get off on the right foot with breastfeeding. Use the log in the appendix to record your baby's feeds and diapers. That will give you, your doctor and your lactation consultant a clear picture of how breastfeeding is going.

Engorgement

One of the earliest problems that many mothers encounter is engorgement. When your milk begins to make the transition from colostrum to mature milk sometime between days 3 and 5, you will experience very full breasts. Fullness is normal. However, if your breasts become hard and tender, and your baby is unable to grasp your nipple, they have become engorged. The key to preventing engorgement is frequent nursing. If you nurse your baby every 2 – 3 hours, there is much less likelihood that you will have problems with engorgement.

Usually if your baby has been latching on correctly and nursing well, you will not experience painfully engorged breasts. If your breasts do become engorged, however, you will need to soften them in order to be able to feed your baby. You have several options available to you.

• Get in a hot shower and allow the water to flow over your breasts. Massage them until the milk begins to flow and they soften. As soon as you get out of the shower, nurse your baby while the milk is flowing.

• If you can't take a shower, try applying warm moist compresses to your breasts and massage until the milk begins to flow and they soften. Or you can dangle your breasts in a bowl of comfortable warm water.

• A good breast pump can help to remove some of the milk once your breasts have been softened by the compresses.

• After feeding you can apply cold compresses to your breasts for comfort. Some studies have indicated that using cold cabbage leaves as described in chapter 6 does help to reduce engorgement. Be careful not to leave the cabbage leaves on for more than about 20 minutes at a time, though, because they can reduce your milk supply.

• You can also take an anti-inflammatory pain reliever such as ibuprofen. This medication is safe for breastfeeding mothers.

Breast Massage and Hand Expression

Knowing how to massage your breasts will prove indispensable if you ever do get engorged or find yourself in an emergency situation where you are unable to nurse. If you can massage your breasts when you are engorged, it will be easier to get your milk flowing. Use the following technique to massage your breasts. Always begin with clean hands.

• Use moist heat prior to massage

• Support your breast with one hand.

• Massage with your fingertips making small circles all around the outer periphery of your breast moving in toward the areola.

Make sure to include the region under your arm because that is breast tissue, too.

• Using your fingertips or the palm of your hand stroke firmly but gently from the outside of the breast toward the areola.

• Be certain you massage your entire breast, paying special attention to any area that is particularly firm.

• After you have massaged your breast, you can feed your baby, or you can pump or manually express your milk.

You should learn how to express your milk manually because you probably will encounter situations where you will need to do so. If you plan to collect your milk, make sure that you have washed your hands with antibacterial soap.

• Sit in a comfortable, relaxed position. Remember that part of effective let-down involves your mental state, so it would be helpful to focus on your baby. You can look at his picture or even listen to a tape-recording of his sounds if he isn't right there with you. Meditating on Scripture can also help you to relax.

• Place your thumb above and your first two fingers below your nipple about 2 inches from the tip of the nipple. Gently push in toward your chest wall. Next compress the breast tissue between your thumb and fingers. Then relax your fingers. Don't squeeze! You may just see a drop of milk at first, or you might get a stream. Repeat, rotating your fingers so that you compress ducts all the way around your breast until the flow slows down on the first breast, then express from the other breast.

• If you are using manual expression to empty your breasts, then you will probably express from each breast two or maybe even three times, changing breasts when the flow stops.

Plugged Ducts

Another problem that some mothers experience is plugged ducts which result from milk and/or cast-off cells accumulating within a duct and forming a blockage. You might feel a lump or knot, but this is not always the case. The plug could appear as a very painful small white "blister" on the tip of your nipple. Often a woman who is prone to plugged ducts has an abundant milk supply. The blockage may be caused by incomplete emptying of the breasts, by skipped feedings or by pressure from a bra or other clothing that is too tight. Women who are prone to plugged ducts might want to avoid underwire bras and try not to skip nursings.

Evidence does exist that there may be a link between stress and plugged ducts. Carla had already nursed four previous children when I met her. She was homeschooling her older children as she nursed baby Jay. Over a three month period from November to January, Carla had repeated plugged ducts. She was trying to finish the first semester work with her children, have a big family Thanksgiving, and prepare for out-of-town company coming for Christmas – all while she was nursing her baby. As we talked, she mentioned that she had experienced similar problems with two of her other children. When her plate was too full and her life was filled with stress, she was prone to plugged ducts.

If left untreated, a plugged duct can lead to mastitis. Therefore, it is very important to take the following steps as soon as you realize you have one.

• Nurse as frequently as possible, and do not skip any feedings. Even during the night, you need to nurse at 2-3 hour intervals.

• Take sunflower lecithin, 1 capsule 4 times a day to help emulsify the milk, and rest as much as possible.

• Apply warm moist heat to the breast and gently massage the sore area toward the nipple. Then allow the baby to nurse. Once again, a hot shower will feel wonderful!

• Vary your nursing position frequently. Try sitting cross-legged with baby in your lap, allowing your breast to hang down into baby's mouth. Massage the plug, using as much firm pressure as you can stand, down toward the nipple while you nurse.

• There is some evidence that if you can direct the baby's chin toward the plug, it will help alleviate the situation. This may require some very creative positioning, however, depending upon where the plug is in your breast.

• If you have caked secretions on your nipple openings, rinse gently with warm water to remove them.

Mastitis

Mastitis is the medical name for a breast infection. It is a systemic infection (usually caused Staphylococcus aureus) which involves the entire body. It can result from a plugged duct or from a crack in the nipple through which bacteria have entered. Typical symptoms of mastitis include fever and flu-like general malaise. You may even notice red streaks on your breast. If you notice a reddened, warm, painful area on your breast accompanied by an overall sick feeling, contact your doctor immediately. If you have mastitis, do all of the following:

• Call your doctor. Although some cases of mastitis may resolve within 24-48 hours without antibiotic treatment, you do need to be under a doctor's care. Most doctors will prescribe antibiotics to fight the systemic infection of mastitis.

• Heat helps relieve the discomfort of a breast infection, so apply warm compresses before and during nursing and as frequently as needed for comfort. Following each feed, you can use cold compresses for comfort and to help alleviate the inflammation.

• Nurse frequently! Your baby will not get sick from your milk, and you need to keep your breasts as empty as possible. Sometimes it is excruciatingly painful to nurse when you have mastitis, but keeping the breast as empty as possible is critical to recovery. Some doctors who are not as informed as they should be about breastfeeding still advise mothers to wean when they have mastitis. This is VERY poor advice. Your mastitis is more likely to become a breast abscess if you do not nurse.

Breast Abscess

A breast abscess occurs when an infected area fills with pus. It usually results from mastitis that has either been untreated or ineffectively treated. The breast will have a spot that is painfully tender.

It will usually be red, but sometimes an abscess can be present even without redness. Ultrasound is often needed to provide an accurate diagnosis. When an abscess occurs, it will need to be surgically treated. The abscess must be opened to allow the pus to drain.

Look for a surgeon who has experience treating breastfeeding women who plan to continue nursing. Generally the procedure can be performed under local anesthesia in the office. Make certain the surgeon plans to make his incision as far as possible away from the areola so that breastfeeding won't be compromised. Weaning is almost never necessary when an abscess is treated. In fact, if the surgeon operates in such a way as to protect breastfeeding, the baby can breastfeed as soon as the mother feels comfortable doing so. Even if the mother does have to wean from one breast, she can continue to nurse on the other. It is entirely possible to breastfeed on just one side.

Sore or Cracked Nipples

It is not normal or routine for your nipples to be sore as a result of breastfeeding. If your nipples are hurting, that is an indication that something is wrong. You need to see a lactation specialist to figure out what the problem is. Most problems with sore nipples are caused by poor position or poor latch.

Marilyn's baby Jaclyn was ten days old when Marilyn called me to rent a breast pump. She said her nipples were bleeding, and she was afraid the blood would be bad for her baby. When I visited her and saw how Jaclyn was latching on, I understood why Marilyn's nipples were cracked and scabbed over. Marilyn was holding Jaclyn too far away from her body with her tummy facing up. Jaclyn was only getting about an inch of nipple in her mouth, and she was pulling and tugging. Correcting her positioning and Jaclyn's latch certainly made a difference. Nevertheless, Marilyn did end up using the breast pump for a few days in order to let her nipples heal. She used finger feeding to give her breast milk to Jaclyn.

If you do have sore nipples, try the following:

- Be sure the baby is correctly positioned. If you are using a cradle hold, he needs to be tummy to tummy and pulled in close. You shouldn't be hunched over him. Rather, put a pillow under him to bring him up to your breast level.

• Be sure he is latched on correctly. He needs to have as much areola in his mouth as possible. Don't allow him to latch onto the tip of the nipple, then slide onto the areola. Make sure he opens his mouth wide before you let him latch on.

• Make sure that he is sucking correctly with his tongue out over his lower gum. If you feel his lower gum against your breast, he is not nursing correctly. You may need to pull his chin down after he latches on in order to help him bring his tongue out. If he is sucking improperly, you need to have a lactation specialist work with you and your baby to help him learn to suck correctly.

• Never use any ointment on your nipples except medical grade lanolin or a specifically designed nipple cream unless prescribed by a doctor or recommended by a lactation consultant. Other ointments must either be washed off or could potentially cause allergic reactions in the baby. The best medicine for sore nipples may well be your own milk. After each feeding, gently blot baby's saliva off your nipple. Express a small amount of milk and rub it into your nipple, allowing it to air dry before you close your bra. You may also express milk and rub it into your nipple between feedings. Your milk has factors that will fight off infection.

• Be sure to keep your nipples as dry as possible. Make sure your bra pads do not have plastic or nylon liners. The best pads are cotton. (To help stop leaking, apply pressure directly to your nipple, either by crossing your arms tightly or directly with your fingers.) Change bra pads frequently.

• Wear breast shells underneath your bra to allow the air to circulate around your nipple and to help the healing process. Be sure that you purchase shells with a wide base.

• Vary your baby's nursing position to ease the stress on the sorest part of the nipple.

• It is helpful to express some milk before your baby latches on, so that you will have let-down and his initial suck won't be as vigorous.

• If your nipples are badly cracked or are bleeding, you might want to rent a hospital quality pump for a few days and feed your baby expressed milk. A lactation specialist can help you adjust the pump so that it will be more comfortable than actually nursing while you allow your nipples to heal. But remember, the goal is to correct the problem that caused your sore nipples in the first place and get the baby back to the breast as quickly as possible.

Tongue-tie

Sometimes a short frenulum (the little band of tissue under the tongue) can also cause extremely painful nipples. This condition is known as "tongue-tie" or ankyloglossia. In years past, doctors routinely clipped a tight frenulum to improve speech development; however, research showed this condition doesn't affect speech. So now many physicians are unwilling to perform this simple procedure. A lactation consultant can tell you if your baby has this condition. Typically a baby with a short frenulum is unable to extend his tongue over his bottom gum line. His tongue may appear to have sort of a heart shape. If your baby does have this condition, ask your lactation consultant to recommend a pediatrician who is supportive of breastfeeding and would be willing to perform a frenulectomy.

Jorge was nearly two months old when I first saw his mother Andrea nurse him. She was concerned that he cried all the time and didn't seem to be full after eating. His pediatrician was telling Andrea she had to give him formula because he wasn't gaining enough weight. Nevertheless, he did have sufficient wet and soiled diapers. The instant Jorge opened his mouth, I knew what was wrong. He had an extremely short frenulum and wasn't able to nurse well enough to get the hindmilk he needed. In Peru few pediatricians were willing to perform a frenulectomy; however, the Lord led me to a wonderful professor of pediatrics who was happy to see Jorge and Andrea the next morning. After the quick clip, Jorge latched on and nursed better than he ever had. He became a different baby and quickly gained weight.

Thrush

When a mother has been nursing comfortably for several weeks or months, then suddenly begins to have sore nipples, she may have a yeast infection (candida albicans), also known as "thrush." The pain from thrush does not diminish after latch-on; in fact, sometimes it continues even after the baby has stopped nursing. The nipples may have a red or dark pink irritated appearance, or look very dry, and the mother may report that they are itchy or have a burning sensation. However, thrush might be present without any external symptoms at all. Another common symptom of thrush is shooting pain deep within the breast after or between feedings. Some mothers report it as pain in the area under their arms (the axilla); others describe a pain shooting through the chest wall toward the back. If you are having these symptoms, then you and your baby both need to be treated.

Babies can have thrush in their mouths, as well. It looks like little white patches inside their cheeks and lips or on the roof of the mouth. Some babies don't have any symptoms in their mouths, but have a red, angry looking diaper rash that is caused by candida. Whether the baby has any symptoms or not, however, both mother and infant must be treated to prevent the recurrence of thrush.

Your doctor can prescribe an antifungal cream for your breasts as well as an antifungal gel for your baby's mouth. However, one of the oldest and quickest (and messiest) treatments is gentian violet. Apply the Gentian Violet to your nipple and areola with a q-tip once a day right before nursing. After feeding, baby's mouth will be purple as well. One treatment a day should resolve the problem within a week.

Dr. Jack Newman recommends an All Purpose Nipple Ointment which must be compounded by a pharmacist. The ingredients include the following:

- Mupiricin
- Betamathasone

• Micanazole (flucanazole may be substituted)

For more information on his excellent thrush protocol, see http://home.bflrc.com/newman/handouts/0501-HR_C-Candida_Protocol.htm

Occasionally the yeast infection will be intraductal which requires a systemic treatment. Flucanazol (Diflucan) is widely recognized as an effective treatment for systemic yeast. An initial dose of 200-400 grams followed by at least 2 – 3 weeks of 100 grams a day has been shown to provide long-term relief from candidiasis. The treatment must continue until you have been symptom free for 7 days.

Dianna had been exclusively breastfeeding Margaret Rose for four months when she was first referred to me because of her ongoing nipple pain. Although they had gotten off to a rocky start, Dianna and Margaret Rose had been doing fairly well, although Diana couldn't ever remember a time when nursing had been completely pain-free. Even after Margaret Rose finished nursing, Dianna felt an ongoing ache deep within her breasts. Topical yeast treatments helped some, but didn't completely relieve her pain. Diflucan was a relatively new treatment at that time, and I had never read or heard about it. However, Dianna began seeing a different doctor who recognized the signs of systemic yeast and began her on a 2 week course of Diflucan. Within a week, Dianna reported significant improvement in her symptoms, and by the time she finished her course of treatment, she showed no evidence whatsoever of any candida infection.

Poor weight gain/Low milk supply

During the first two months babies should gain about an ounce a day. By the third month, that weight gain will slow down to about a half-ounce a day. If breastfeeding is not well established within the first week, milk production problems can result. Research has demonstrated that the earlier and more frequently an infant is put to the breast, the more quickly the mother will have an adequate milk supply. If early breastfeeding must be interrupted, the mother needs to establish her milk supply by double pumping at least 8 times a day with a hospital quality pump.

It is certainly frightening when your baby isn't gaining enough weight. When a baby is not gaining weight adequately, many doctors will immediately suggest that the mother supplement with formula. In some cases, supplementation will be necessary; however, a lactation consultant should be seen to figure out what the problem is with the breastfeeding. The following suggestions will help get more of your own milk into your baby:

• Make certain that the baby is positioned correctly and latching on well.

• As the baby nurses massage your breasts, massaging the milk down toward the nipple and into his mouth.

• Go to bed with your baby for a day or two and nurse as frequently as you can, giving the baby unrestricted access to the breast.

• Be sure you are eating well and drinking sufficient water.

• If your baby is sleepy and doesn't seem interested in nursing, undress him down to his diaper, and keep him next to your body. Take off your bra when you nurse for maximum skin-to-skin contact.

• If you do need to supplement, do it at your breast with a nursing supplementer. Medela's Supplemental Nursing System (SNS) or the Lactaid nursing supplementer allow your baby to receive supplementary formula or expressed breastmilk while he is nursing at your breast. You do need a trained specialist to make sure you are using it correctly.

• Following each feed, pump your breasts to provide further stimulation. Pump for about five minutes on one side, switch to the other for the same period of time, then repeat both breasts.

Galactagogues

You may want to use a galactagogue – a substance which you take to increase your milk supply. Fenugreek is a natural galactagogue that many mothers have found effective; however, you may find that you smell a bit like maple syrup after taking it! Motherlove sells several herbal supplements which include fenugreek, blessed thistle, and fennel leaf extracts, all of which have been demonstrated to help increase milk supply. Another supplement, Goat's Rue, has actually been shown to help increase glandular tissue for mothers whose breasts did not change during pregnancy. Mother's Milk Tea also contains several natural components. Ovaltine contains whey which also helps boost milk supply. Finally, oatmeal is another natural galactagogue,

Two prescription drugs have proven to be very helpful in increasing milk supply: Metaclopramide (Reglan) and Domperidone (Motilium). Unfortunately, Domperidone is not currently available in the United States. Metaclopramide works by increasing prolactin production; however, it can have some unpleasant side effects. Either of these drugs is a last resort. Nevertheless, if you are doing all of the other things listed above, then using a prescription drug may be just what it takes to augment your milk production. For more information see Making More Milk by Diana West, IBCLC and Lisa Morasco, IBCLC (2008, McGraw and Hill)

Press on

It can be terribly discouraging when you have any kind of breastfeeding problem. Remember Paul's words in Phil. 4:13,"I can do all things through Him who strengthens me." Breastfeeding fits into the category of "all things." God designed you to provide the nutrition your baby needs. He designed your baby to thrive on your milk. When you begin to feel discouraged, anxious, or frustrated, go to the Lord in prayer. Pour out your worries and hurt at His feet. Ask Him for wisdom in resolving your problems.

A lactation consultant, particularly one who shares your faith, can be one of the most valuable members of your health care team. Never hesitate to call her with any questions or concerns you have. If you call when you first notice a potential problem, you may be able to avert a more serious situation. Not only will your lactation consultant help you resolve your problem in its beginning stages, she will also be your cheerleader. Every new mother needs a cheerleader, so let your LC get you all "pumped up" to be the best nursing mother you can be!

Chapter 8:

The Breastfeeding Father –
Getting Dad Involved

*Do nothing from selfishness or empty conceit, but
with humility of mind regard one another as more
important than yourselves; do not merely look out
for your own personal interests, but also for the
interests of others.*

– Philippians 2:3-4

"Honey, I'm so tired. Do you think you could help with the dishes tonight while I nurse Daniel?" I asked as I wearily dropped into my favorite nursing chair in the living room. After a long summer day with three year old Sarah, who, as I mentioned earlier, was incredibly strong-willed, and three month old Daniel, I was exhausted. My husband was pretty busy, too, as the solo pastor of a small-town church with an elderly congregation. Nevertheless, to me he was Superman as he cleaned the kitchen up so I could sit, relax, and nurse my son.

Dad, you will play a critical role in your wife's successful breastfeeding experience. The decision to breastfeed is so much more than just a matter of infant feeding. It is truly a parenting style that both parents embrace. You are the God-ordained head of your household, so it is your responsibility to pray for wisdom as you seek to parent the baby that God gives you. James 1:5 says, "But if any of you lacks wisdom, let him ask of God, who gives to all generously and without reproach, and it will be given to him."

Breastfeeding benefits for Dad

Take time to learn all you can about breastfeeding. You might begin by reading through this book with your wife. In addition, there are some very specific benefits of breastfeeding that you as a father will enjoy.

• You'll get more sleep since you don't have to get up to feed a crying baby in the middle of the night. Just keep your baby in a bassinet by your bed, or even in the bed next to your wife, and you'll sleep straight through the night.

• You'll save money – lots of it! For starters, you will save about $200/month on formula. Some infant formulas may be a little less expensive, and some may be quite a bit more. Because breastfed babies have fewer ear infections, upper respiratory infections and gastrointestinal infections, you will also save money on doctor's bills and prescriptions.

• Your wife will get her pre-pregnancy figure back more rapidly. Although they still need to "eat for two," breastfeeding women tend to lose the extra weight gained during pregnancy faster than their formula-feeding counterparts. The hormone oxytocin which controls the release of milk also causes her uterus to get back to its regular size quickly.

• You will have a baby who learns early that he can trust. When your wife feeds him on cue, he will develop a sense of security about his world. He won't have to cry all the time to make his needs known. Some babies are fussier than others, but even a baby with a more sensitive, high-need nature will be calmer and easier to handle if he is fed on cue. A baby who learns to trust while still at the breast will grow into a young person who is able to understand what it means to trust his Heavenly Father.

• You will have the reward of knowing that you have supported your wife in providing the very best possible start in life for your child. Not only does breastfeeding provide antibodies and immunities to keep your baby healthy, it also helps his brain to develop better. Research indicates that breastfed babies have higher IQs.

How you can help

Some fathers believe that unless they are involved in feeding their baby, they can't really do anything to help. That is FAR from the truth. Nevertheless, once breastfeeding is established, Dad CAN help feed by giving bottles of expressed breastmilk, if Mom wants him to. Sometimes having that bottle for Dad to give allows his wife a much-needed get away to the mall or to a restaurant with a friend.

Still, there are many other ways that you can be directly involved with your baby's care even if you never feed him. Fathers tend to interact with their babies in a more playful way than mothers. Even from the earliest moments, Dad, you have a unique and special role in your baby's life. Here are some specific ways you can be involved with him.

• Bathtime can be a special time for you and your little one. You can be the one who takes charge of bathing your baby and even make that a special part of your bedtime routine with him. By taking on this job, you kill two birds with one stone: you give your wife a much-needed break from her 24 hour a day job, and you build a special bond with your baby. When Daniel, and later John Carl, got to be about 4 or 5 months old, my husband began taking Daddy-baby baths with them. They loved it!

• When your baby is especially fussy or has colic, you can put him in a sling and go for a walk with him. Hold him up against your chest with his head tucked up under your chin. Sing or talk to him as you walk, and you will find that the tone and rhythm of your voice will soothe him pretty quickly. This could become an evening ritual for the two of you.

• Learn to change diapers. Believe me, your wife will appreciate your help in this area more than you can begin to imagine! Then when she is nursing and the baby decides to fill his britches in the middle of his meal, you can be Johnny-on-the-spot.

• Be your baby's favorite teddy bear and most fun playmate. Playing with your baby will stimulate his senses and encourage his development. Learn specific age-appropriate ways of playing with your baby; you will both benefit from the time you share together.

• Read to your baby. This is another way that you can use your voice to entertain and fascinate your baby. Colorful pictures combined with your deep voice will make story time with Daddy a favorite time of day for your baby. As he gets older, your baby may meet you at the door, book in hand, begging for you to read to him.

TLC for your wife

Your wife needs some special tender loving care during the first few weeks postpartum. Her job is to care for and nurse your baby. Your primary job during these days is to take good care of her and make sure that she knows how much you love her and how proud of her you are. Here are some specific things you can do to give your wife that TLC she needs:

• When she sits down to nurse, bring her a glass of water, juice or herbal tea. She will appreciate the fluids because nursing tends to make moms thirsty.

• Offer a relaxing massage if she is tense. One of the things that inhibits milk production is stress. However, if you can massage her upper back and shoulders to help relieve some of her tension, she will have an easier time nursing. Her milk will let-down more readily, and she may even produce more milk.

• Draw a warm bubble bath for her, light candles and put on soothing music. The object at this point is not romance, but relaxation.

• Run interference for her when well-meaning friends or relatives stop by unannounced. If she just isn't up to seeing people, then it's up to you to kindly, but gently, let them know that this isn't a good time for a visit.

• If friends or relatives (especially yours) criticize her nursing, go to bat for her without having to be asked. If you are convinced that she is doing the best thing for your baby, the strength of that confidence will give you the ability to say what needs to be said.

• If you have other children, be especially sensitive to their needs. The less demand they place on Mommy, the more of herself she will have to give to your new baby. Help them understand that the baby won't always be so demanding of Mommy's time.

• Realize that housework can wait. She may not mop, vacuum, wash windows and scrub baseboards like she used to. If you can afford it, the first few months after your baby is born, hire someone to help with the housework. If you can't then pitch in yourself.

• Understand that she may not have meals ready on time. Baby needs to eat when he is hungry. You do too, but baby hasn't learned to be patient, and you have! If you have culinary skills, now is definitely the time to employ them!

• Put your foot down and help your wife say "NO" to being overcommitted. If she is the kind of person who is on every committee at church and involved in half a dozen other things, you may have to help her realize that she is entering a new season of life when she may have to scale back on some of her obligations.

Remember that Jesus came not to be served, but to serve. You would do well to follow His example! Look for practical ways you can serve your wife on a daily basis. As she sees you loving her in the way that Christ loved the church and making sacrifices for her, her respect and admiration for you will deepen.

Romance reality

The addition of a family member does change the dynamics of your relationship. However, that change does NOT have to be a negative thing. You will have added stress in your life; on the other hand, you will also have a new source of joy that can draw you closer to each other than you've ever been. As you lovingly serve your wife during this period, you will find that you achieve a deeper level of intimacy than ever before.

During the early post-partum period, your wife's body is recovering from childbirth. Normally it will be about six weeks before she is ready to resume sexual relations. That doesn't mean, though, that she won't need you to hold her and show her how much you love her in other ways. When she is ready to resume relations, you may find that she needs a vaginal lubricant for comfort; sometimes during lactation vaginal secretions decrease.

Dads occasionally feel that the breasts are now off limits since they are being used to feed the baby. That isn't the case at all. Some breastfeeding women do feel all "touched out" and don't really want their husbands to fondle their breasts right now. Find out what your wife wants. Don't be surprised if milk leaks while you are making love. The same hormones that are involved in sex are involved in breastfeeding. You might even want to take a taste… it is sweeter than cow's milk and you'll see why your baby likes it so much.

Many hormonal changes will occur in your wife's body after she gives birth and begins nursing. Many women experience mild feelings of depression in the first days and weeks after having a baby. These "baby blues" as they are called are normal. However, if your wife seems to be sinking into a lethargic, all-consuming state of depression, please take her to the doctor. She may need pharmacological help to enable her to deal with the hormonal changes she is experiencing. Certain anti-depressants can be taken while breastfeeding. According to Dr. Thomas Hale, the preferred medications are Zoloft, Paxil, and Celexa in that order. For more information on this postpartum depression visit http://www.granitescientific.com/.

This season of your life will pass quickly. Before you know it, your newborn will be taking his first steps. Then he'll be learning to ride a bicycle and heading off to school. Then before you know it, he'll be going on his first date. Your role in his life is critical to shaping his view of God. A child who grows up with a dad who is involved with him and actively shows his love for him has a tremendous advantage. He is able to relate to his Heavenly Father as a caring, loving Being.

However, as important as your relationship with your child is, your relationship with his mother is even more important. The most secure children are those who grow up knowing that their parents love each other and love them. The greatest gift you can give to your child is to love his mother. He needs to see that you are absolutely head-over-heels in love with her and committed to her for life. Show your little guy that you are crazy about his mom, and he'll have a great model for his own life. If you have a daughter, someday she'll look for a boy who loves her the way you loved her mom. What you do now will truly have a lasting impact!

Chapter 9:

You Need Mothering –
Special Encouragement for Grandmothers

"Let no unwholesome word proceed from your mouth, but only such a word as is good for edification according to the need of the moment, so that it will give grace to those who hear."

– Ephesians 4:29

As I worked with Anita in the hospital, her mother kept telling her that she needed to give the baby a bottle. Anita had planned to exclusively breastfeed, and there were no bottles of formula in the crib, so she kept asking nurses to bring in bottles. However, that wasn't what Anita wanted, and her baby was nursing beautifully with good pees and poops. Therefore, nobody brought any bottles, and I tried to help the new grandmother understand how breastfeeding works.

Successfully nursing your baby involves your mental attitude toward breastfeeding. Surrounding yourself with friends and family members who support and encourage you will help you have a positive outlook and contribute to your success. Your mother and mother-in-law are two people who can have a definite impact on your breastfeeding experience. If they are positive and support- ive of breastfeeding, it will be much easier for you. You need to recognize, though, that many women in their generation may not have breastfed. Perhaps they didn't have the information available to them that you have, or maybe nobody ever encouraged them to nurse. However, you can help them understand what a gift you are giving their grandchild by having them read the following section that is written just for them. Feel free to photocopy this chapter for your mother and mother-in-law (and any aunts, grandmothers or sisters who might need to read these words, too.)

A Very Special Grandmother

Congratulations! Your daughter or daughter-in-law has chosen to give your new grandbaby the very best start in life! Maybe she is following the example that you set when you breastfed. Or perhaps you didn't breastfeed and are wondering why she has made this de- cision. By taking the time to read this section of the book, you will gain two very important things: first, you will gain an understand- ing of why she has decided to nurse and how breastfeeding works, and secondly, you will learn how you can support and encourage her as she nurtures your precious grandchild.

WHY BREASTFEED?

Although there are a multitude of benefits covered in chapter 2, here I will focus on four specific reasons why your grandbaby's mom has decided to nurse him.

Breastmilk is the ideal infant food.

One of the primary reasons that many mothers decide to breastfeed is because breastmilk is the perfect food for babies. It changes as a baby grows to meet his changing needs. Your grand- baby will also receive all sorts of nutrients and immunities that no formula could provide. At birth all babies have some immuno- logical protection from their mothers, but only the breastfed baby receives ongoing protection from disease and infection via the immunoglobulins in his mother's milk. Over 100 nutrients, amino acids and other important factors have been identified in mother's milk. Researchers have even found substances in breast milk that aid in the development of brain cells. No formula of human design even comes close to providing all of the benefits of breastmilk!

Breastfeeding is convenient and inexpensive.

For a young couple on a tight budget, formula-feeding may be prohibitive. Breastfeeding is a wonderful way to save a lot of money. Furthermore, because breastfed babies are healthier, their parents also have fewer medical bills. An added benefit is that your grandbaby's mother won't have to concern herself with mixing formula, sterilizing bottles and making sure she heats the baby's formula to just the right temperature.

Breastfeeding provides wonderful bonding opportunities

Breastfed babies bond closely with their mothers, trusting them to meet their needs. This security they experience lays the foundation for later independence. It also provides a basis for their later understanding of the trust they can have in their Heavenly Father. Certainly formula-fed babies can bond with their mothers, too; nevertheless a unique and precious intimacy exists between the breastfed baby and his mother.

Breastfeeding is God's perfect design for infant feeding

God equipped mothers with the means to provide adequate nourishment for their infants for at least the first six months of life. In his perfect plan for creation, He fashioned the breastfeeding relationship to meet the needs of both mother and infant. Your daughter or daughter-in-law will have less risk of pre-menopausal breast cancer and osteoporosis because she has breastfed your grandbaby. Your grandchild is richly blessed to have a mother who wants to nurse him according to God's plan!

How It Works

The first and most important thing you can do is learn all you can about breastfeeding. The following facts will help you understand the breastfeeding process.

• Breastmilk is produced on a supply and demand basis. Therefore, the more a baby nurses, the more milk his mother will produce.

• To produce adequate milk, the mother needs to get sufficient rest.

• Breastmilk is easy to digest, so breastfed babies need to nurse every two or three hours during the day. Typically, an infant should nurse eight to twelve times in a 24 hour period.

• A breastfed baby should not have a bottle or a pacifier for the first four weeks of his life. Sucking on an artificial nipple may confuse him and lead him to temporarily reject his mother's breast.

• Stress, worry or fatigue may affect the hormonal reactions that control let-down. This means that a mother's milk will not be as available to her baby as it needs to be. It also means that her baby will not get the high calorie hindmilk that lets down after ten to 12 minutes.

• Babies go through several growth spurts during which they nurse much more frequently than normal. It is not uncommon during a growth spurt for a baby to nurse every hour and a half. The baby is helping his mother increase her milk supply to meet his growing needs. Typical growth spurt times include ten days, six weeks, 3 months, and six months. Growth spurts may last four to six days.

• Breastfed babies do not need any other type of nourishment for at least the first six months of their lives. Some babies may show an interest in solid foods at around 5 months of age. If a baby can sit up and is able to eat without thrusting the food out with his tongue, he may be ready for solids.

YOUR ROLE

Now you know why your daughter or daughter-in-law has chosen to breastfeed. You also have a basic understanding of how the breastfeeding relationship works. There are several very important things you can do to help ensure that your grandbaby gets the very best possible start in life.

Be a Barnabas

When many in the early church were reluctant to trust the newly converted Paul, Barnabas (whose name means "Son of Encouragement") stepped in as his number one cheerleader. He stood up for Paul and encouraged him to do what God had called him to do. Your job is to be like Barnabas for your daughter or daughter-in law.

One of the most important things that you can do for your grandbaby is to avoid negative and unsupportive comments to his mother about the way she is feeding him. If you did not breastfeed, or your nursing experience wasn't very positive, you may tend to think it won't work for her either. If she is surrounded by discouragement, breastfeeding will be difficult. The let-down reflex is dependent, to a great extent, upon the mother's emotional condition. Worry, fear and stress may very well interfere with her breastfeeding successfully.

Don't expect your breastfed grandchild to have the same kind of structured feeding schedule that a bottle fed baby may have. Encourage his mother to go ahead and feed him if he seems hungry. One of the most helpful things you can do is to praise your grandchild's mother. Be sure to let her know you think she is doing a good job. Take every opportunity to cheer her on.

Mother the new mother

During the first few weeks after she gives birth, your daughter or daughter-in-law has one very important job: taking care of her baby. If this is her first baby, she may feel very unsure of herself in this new role. It might be tempting for her to let you do everything, especially if you are a take-charge sort of person. But please don't let her do that. Try to avoid caring for the new baby yourself; instead encourage the new mother and reassure her of her own abilities. One of the greatest gifts you can give her is a sense of confidence in her own maternal role.

Do look for ways that you can pamper the new mother. You might cook for her or do the laundry. Perhaps you can help by going shopping for her. If she has other children, this can be a very special time for you to focus on them, as well. She may ask you to help in specific ways; do so graciously and willingly. The most important thing here is that you find ways to help her get the rest her body needs to recover from childbirth and to make the milk your grandbaby needs.

Try to be especially sensitive to your daughter or daughter-in-law's feelings regarding the establishment of her new family .If you live out of town, find out when would be the best time for you to come. She might want you there as soon as the baby is born. On the other hand, she might prefer that you wait for a week or two and then come. If both sets of grandparents live out of town, it would be very wise to coordinate your visits so that the new family has help for the longest time possible. Perhaps the mother's parents can come right when the baby is born and stay for a week or two. Then the father's parents can visit when the baby is a couple of weeks old.

Pray for your grandbaby and his mother

This is the most priceless gift you can give them. If she can be certain that you are daily asking God to give her wisdom and encouragement, your daughter or daughter-in-law will be blessed indeed. Even now (after 38 years of marriage) my mother-in-law still tells me nearly every time we talk that she is praying for us and our children. I am so richly blessed to have a mother-in-law who brings us before the throne of grace each day. Her mother set that example for her, and she is continuing in that intercessory role. Ultimately, you long for your grandbaby to come into a lifelong relationship with Christ. As you love and pray for your grandbaby and his parents, you will be a very special grandmother indeed!

Chapter 10:

Hang On! Help Is on the Way –
Finding a Support System

"Bear one another's burdens, and thereby fulfill the law of Christ."

– Galatians 6:2

Pilar came from an upper class Peruvian home where none of the women had ever breastfed. The cultural norm for Pilar was to have a nanny care for the baby so that the new mother could resume her busy social life. However, Pilar had studied in the United States and seen that breastfeeding was the norm for many well-educated American women. When Jorge Luis was born, Pilar was determined to nurse, regardless of the obstacles. However, that wasn't as easy as it seemed because everyone close to her, including her pediatrician who was an old family friend, discouraged her. In fact, her pediatrician even believed that Peruvian women weren't physiologically capable of producing enough milk for their babies!

When she first learned about our support group for breastfeeding mothers, Pilar couldn't believe that there was actually a place she could go to receive advice and encouragement. As she began to learn more about breastfeeding, her confidence in her own ability to provide for Jorge Luis grew. Her mother and sister couldn't believe how well he was growing on just her breastmilk. Jorge Luis went on to exclusively breastfeed for six months, despite his pediatrician's insistence that he should start solids at four months. He continued nursing into his second year of life and was notably healthier than his formula-fed cousins!

BUILDING YOUR SUPPORT NETWORK

You need to surround yourself with people who will uphold and encourage you as you nurse your baby. You have chosen to parent your baby in a manner that you believe is Biblical. However, you may have some people in your circle of close friends who disagree with your choices. When friends try to tell you that you should just give your baby formula, or your baby is nursing too often, or breastfeeding is too demanding, they are setting you up for failure. You may have to temporarily distance yourself from those who discourage you.

Even before you give birth, find other breastfeeding mothers with whom you can network. You might become part of a breastfeeding support group while you are still pregnant. Attend meetings and learn all you can. Observe other mothers with their babies. Listen to the questions they ask and the answers that various members offer. Read all you can and watch any videos that your group leader has. When your baby is born, let your group leader know. Don't hesitate to call her if you have any concerns once you and the baby come home.

Friends

Look at your circle of acquaintances – people you know from work, from church, from the neighborhood. Who do you know who has breastfed? Don't be shy about asking women you know how nursing went for them. Find two or three women who had successful and enjoyable breastfeeding relationships with their babies and begin to build a closer friendship with them. Having good friends who are sold on breastfeeding will make it easier for you if you have any difficulty. Your friends will be there to cheer you on and encourage you through the rough times.

If your best friends think breastfeeding is bothersome or that formula is just as good as breastmilk, you may need to avoid them in the early days of your baby's life. When the people closest to you are telling you that you won't succeed or that it isn't worth it, you will grow discouraged and may give up during the first few weeks. On the other hand, if you have a few friends you can call who believe in you and your ability to nurture your baby, you will be encouraged to stick with it, even when you feel frustrated.

Your Church Family

Many churches have popularized a parenting series that glorifies parenting by schedule. The Growing Kids God's Way program has some good information about discipline and raising kids who are well-mannered. However, early editions of the Preparation for Parenthood book (now called Babywise) cautioned mothers against nursing on demand. Mothers are taught that they shouldn't rely on "maternal instinct"; rather, they should watch the clock and not give in when an infant is crying. In several documented instances, babies nursed according to this advice ended up in the hospital because of failure to thrive. One infant I saw at two weeks of age never cried, and rarely awakened to nurse. He was too dehydrated and weak. I had his mother take him to the emergency room immediately where he was admitted and remained hospitalized for several days. If you have an edition prior to 2001, you should discard it.

If your church is using this material, be aware that other excellent Christian parenting material does exist. Christian Parenting and Child Care by William Sears, M.D. (Nashville: Broadman and Holman Publishers, 1997) is an outstanding resource that every Christian parent needs to keep handy. Within the framework of Biblical truth, Dr. Sears examines the roles of husband and wife, parent and child, and offers a compendium of parenting practices that will ultimately lead a child to be independent, healthy and secure.

You might find that other mothers will be excited to see that there is a solid Biblical alternative to the Growing Kids God's Way material. Perhaps you can form a small group with other like-minded mothers in your congregation to encourage and support one another as you parent your infants. If you can find an experienced mother in the congregation who successfully breastfed her own children, she may be able to act as a mentor for you.

Another way to connect with other young mothers in the church is through the MOPS (Mothers of Preschoolers) program. Although this program is not specifically designed to be a support group for breastfeeding mothers, you may meet other mothers there who will encourage you. Not everyone in your MOPS group will have had a positive breastfeeding experience, though. Therefore, you need to listen as other mothers talk about their experiences and ask the Lord to guide you into friendships with those women who will most encourage you.

FIND A BREASTFEEDING SUPPORT GROUP

Many different kinds of support groups exist for nursing mothers. Some hospitals offer support groups for the mothers who give birth in their facilities. Some private practice lactation consultants have support groups. One of the best known and most widely respected support organizations is La Leche League. With the proliferation of online networking, there is even a breastfeeding support group whose members make their first contact via the internet.

Hospital-based support groups

If your hospital offers the services of a lactation consultant, she should be able to connect you with a good breastfeeding support group. We talked about Baby Friendly Hospitals earlier. Hospitals that have received this designation offer ongoing support to their nursing mothers. Elmbrook Hospital in Milwaukee, WI, for example, offers "The Baby Connection," a group that meets every Wednesday morning. Babies can be weighed each week; moms can bring their questions, and a lactation expert is available to offer help and support.

Some hospitals sponsor community-based support groups that meet in other locations. Brookwood Medical Center in Birmingham, AL, has a program called Best Start. They have meetings every week at three different locations throughout the city. At each meeting a lactation consultant is available to answer questions and offer support to new mothers. They also have a scale available so that mothers can see how their infants are gaining.

Some hospitals use peer counselors to offer support and assistance. Mothers who have successfully breastfed and been a part of the hospital's program for a period of time may be asked to serve as mentors for new mothers. At Rush-Presbyterian St. Luke's Medical Center in Chicago, IL, they have five women whose children range in age from 9 months to 6 years serving as peer counselors for their Rush Mother's Milk Club program. Each of these women has successfully nursed an infant who was in the neo-natal intensive care unit. They offer tremendous encouragement to other mothers who are facing very challenging situations.

Community-based support groups

In different parts of the country, various kinds of groups exist for nursing mothers. For example, in parts of Delaware, Maryland and Pennsylvania, mothers can contact Nursing Mothers Inc., a non-profit organization dedicated to providing mother-to-mother support by trained counselors. Often an IBCLC in private practice may run a support group. To find these resources ask at your hospital, your pediatrician or obstetrician's office, local maternity stores, or check on the internet. To find an IBCLC near you, go to the following site: http://www.iblce.org/US%20registry.htm

Each group will reflect the personality of its leader and members. You might find that some groups that don't feel comfortable for you. Visit various groups and see where you get the most information and support. Often a support group may meet in a church facility. You might find that many of the women in the group share your faith and your values. However, that is not always the case; so take your time as you evaluate what group is best for you.

La Leche League

La Leche League was founded in 1956 by seven mothers in Franklin Park, IL, who were concerned about the lack of support for breastfeeding. At that time the breastfeeding rate had dropped to about 20% in the United States. These women wanted to support and encourage other mothers as they went against the prevailing tide of formula feeding and nursed their infants. Over the years La Leche League has become an international force in breastfeeding advocacy.

The League has as its basic philosophy the following tenets:

• Mothering through breastfeeding is the most natural and effective way of understanding and satisfying the needs of the baby.

• Mother and baby need to be together early and often to establish a satisfying relationship and an adequate milk supply.

• In the early years the baby has an intense need to be with his mother which is as basic as his need for food.

• Breast milk is the superior infant food.

• For the healthy, full-term baby, breast milk is the only food necessary until the baby shows signs of needing solids, about the middle of the first year after birth.

• Ideally the breastfeeding relationship will continue until the baby outgrows the need.

• Alert and active participation by the mother in childbirth is a help in getting breastfeeding off to a good start.

• Breastfeeding is enhanced and the nursing couple sustained by the loving support, help, and companionship of the baby's father. A father's unique relationship with his baby is an important element in the child's development from early infancy.

• Good nutrition means eating a well-balanced and varied diet of foods in as close to their natural state as possible.

• From infancy on, children need loving guidance which reflects acceptance of their capabilities and sensitivity to their feelings. (taken from the La Leche League website http://www.lalecheleague.org/philosophy.html)

At La Leche League meetings mothers receive instruction in basic breastfeeding technique, help with problem solving, advice on weaning and nutrition, and general support in parenting. The leaders can complete a training program in order to qualify as peer counselors. Not only are they required to learn about the anatomy and physiology of breastfeeding and how to solve a wide array of problems, but they must also learn some basic counseling skills so that they can facilitate group meetings.

The first La Leche League meeting I went to when Sarah was a newborn was very encouraging to me. We had struggled some with nursing, despite the wonderful support I was receiving from my lactation consultant. The mothers at La Leche League were very reassuring to me, and I was so grateful. However, I will never forget my shock as I saw a child who must have been about two years old walk over to his mother, pull up her shirt, and begin to nurse. Eventually I did end up nursing each child at least that long; nevertheless, it was a real surprise to me to see it at that meeting. Some mothers may be put off by seeing older babies nursing. If you do find that disconcerting, just remember that you are taking your nursing relationship with your own infant one day at a time. Don't worry about what will happen when he is two!

Mommy Milk Meet-Up

This relatively new phenomenon is growing by leaps and bounds. Groups exist in California, Ohio, Alabama, Texas, North Carolina and Canada, as well as in Moscow, Russia. Moms meet and join via the internet, but actually meet in person for support and encouragement. Often a lactation expert will be involved. Sometimes, however, the support is simply mother-to-mother. For more information, go to http://mommymilk.meetup.com/groups/

Don't just wait around - find somebody to encourage you!

It might be confusing at first as you look at all the possibilities for finding breastfeeding support. However, don't let the wide variety of options deter you. On the other hand, you may be having a very difficult time finding anybody else at all who is breastfeeding in your area. Get on-line. Call your doctor. Check area newspapers for announcements about meetings. Find other moms who have the same values and commitments that you have, and get busy building each other up!

Chapter 11:

Hi Ho, Hi Ho, It's Off to Work We Go –
Solutions for Moms in the Workplace

"She considers a field and buys it; out of her earn-
ings she plants a vineyard. She sets about her work
vigorously; her arms are strong for her tasks. She
sees that her trading is profitable, and her lamp does
not go out at night."

– Proverbs 31:16-18

Tracy first called me because she didn't seem to have enough milk for her two-month-old daughter Gwendolyn. She had just gone back to her demanding job as an engineer at a large Huntsville firm. Her husband Mark was the music minister at a nearby Baptist church. His income just wasn't enough to make ends meet, so Tracy returned to work after a six -week maternity leave.

Gwendolyn had some food allergy problems that made it imperative for Tracy to keep providing breastmilk for her. However, Tracy's supply just seemed to be dwindling. When Tracy began using a hospital grade breast pump and set up a good pumping schedule, she saw a dramatic improvement. She also began using herbal supplements and co-sleeping to help increase her supply. She went on to nurse Gwendolyn for over a year and a half. When Tracy's second baby was born, she and Mark had saved enough money for her to be able to stay home.

Any woman who has ever had a baby will be quick to say that ALL mothers are working mothers. Caring for an infant, a toddler, or an older child is hard work. A mother is a cook, a housekeeper, a maintenance engineer, a teacher, a chauffer, a nurse, and at the end of the day she tries to be the beautiful woman her husband fell in love with. Anyone who thinks that isn't work has never been a mother!

Nevertheless, some mothers do need to have a second job that forces them to be separated from their children for several hours a day. For some women like Tracy, it is financial necessity that drives them to the workplace. Other women simply find a certain level of fulfillment and validation in the workplace that they don't think they will find at home. Some women thrive on communication with other adults. Prior to giving birth many women just can't imagine "staying home and doing nothing all day." Once the baby arrives, they quickly find that they aren't "doing nothing." I've worked with many women who had planned to return to work, then really didn't want to when the time came. Often they return for a short period of time until they can find the financial means to retire.

TAKING CARE OF BABY

Certainly, the ideal person to care for your baby day-in and day-out is you. Nobody loves him more than you do! However, if you can't be with him 24/7, then you need to find someone you feel comfortable with to help you out. There are a variety of child care options. You could have a relative care for him. You could have a nanny come to your home, or take him to someone else's home. Or you could find a day care situation at a church, a local preschool, or even on-site at your business.

Cautiously selecting an in-home caregiver

You might have a relative or a friend who is just longing to have the opportunity to help you care for your baby. Or perhaps you would simply prefer to have your baby remain in his own surroundings. Maybe you've found out about someone who does child-care in her home. Regardless of the situation, there are some things you need to consider.

• Have you seen your prospective caregiver interact with infants?

• Do you know what her parenting philosophy is?

• How many other children does she care for, and how old are they?

• Are you certain that she'll be able to give your baby the attention he deserves?

• If you are thinking about putting your child in someone else's home, you need to find out if that person is licensed by the state to provide childcare.

• You might also want to find out if she is accredited by the National Association for Family Child Care. You can look online at www.nafcc.org to find a list of accredited providers near you.

Two of the most important areas in which you need to feel 100% confident with your caregiver are faith and feeding. First of all, is she a Christian? Will she sing to your baby and read him Bible stories. Will she pray for him? Will her home be a place of peace where his soul can be nourished? Knowing that your child will receive loving care by a godly woman will make it much easier to leave him. Secondly, does she understand how important breastfeeding is to you, and is she willing to follow your feeding instructions? Sometimes an older relative may still see you as a child, and may not see why she has to follow the directions that you give her.

If you have any red flags as you approach the situation, you need to deal with them openly, honestly, and immediately. You might decide that a trial period is a good idea. Provide your caregiver with a written list of expectations, and be sure that she is meeting your expectations. Drop in unannounced occasionally just to see how things are going during the day when you aren't expected to be there. Some parents who have the caregiver come into their own homes even set up video cameras so they can know what is happening when they are gone.

Carefully choosing a day care provider

Infant care is big business. The array of options is dizzying. You can choose a small church-based day care program, or you can select a large national chain day care provider. Perhaps you will be fortunate enough to have an on-site day care at your business. That is a wonderful option for nursing mothers because they can simply go breastfeed their babies when they need to. However, your company may not offer day care on-site. You may still be able to find a day care provider close enough to your place of work that you can at least go at lunch time to nurse.

On the other hand, you may really want your child in a church-based day care setting. Many Christian mothers think that their babies will receive a higher quality of care if Christians are providing it. This may well be true, but regardless of where you are thinking about putting your baby, you need to know what standards they have for their employees. Are all employees in your church day care actually believers? Does the day care provider require employees to have a certain number of college credits in infant and early childhood development? Have all workers submitted to a criminal background check?

The Interview

As you pray for wisdom in this area, you can trust that God will guide you into the very best situation for you and your baby. Make appointments to see several prospective caregivers when you are in the process of choosing. Go during the day when infants and toddler are there so you can see how the workers interact with them. Visit the infant nursery and see for yourself what the ratio of infants to workers is and how the workers care for their tiny charges. Make a list of questions that you will ask during your interview and take notes, recording not only the answers but also your overall impression of the facility.

Be sure to ask about their protocol for breastfed infants. How do they want you to bring your expressed breastmilk? How often do they feed them? If they don't have ready answers, they may not be very familiar with the differences between formula feeding and breastfeeding. You may find yourself in the position of educating them about the importance of properly handling your breastmilk. If they are not willing to work with you in this area, you probably need to look elsewhere.

TAKING CARE OF YOUR LIQUID GOLD

Some mothers refer to their breastmilk as "liquid gold." I've heard two different explanations for this: a) its value to the baby makes it a real treasure; or b) expressing it can be as challenging as mining gold. I prefer the first explanation, because honestly, expressing your milk shouldn't be difficult at all. The key, however, is having a good breastpump. Once you have the right pump, then you need to know how to best store your milk so that it will be of the greatest possible benefit to your baby.

Finding the Right Pump

Many different kinds of breastpumps are available at your local baby store or online. However, before you run out and buy one, you need to consider several things. The first and most important is how often you will be pumping. Assuming that you are returning full-time to the work place, you will probably be pumping at least twice a day, perhaps more often. A manual pump that is great for the mom who only pumps occasionally really won't do the job for a mom who is pumping daily and needs to maintain her supply. The following types of pumps are available:

• Manual or hand-held pumps. The best of these pumps can be operated with one hand so that you can nurse and pump at the same time to take advantage of your let-down reflex while baby is nursing. Examples include the Medela Harmony, the Avent Isis, and the Ameda One-Hand Breast pump.

• Mini-electric or battery-operated single pumps. Unless you are purchasing one made by a company dedicated to researching and providing the best possible breastfeeding equipment, this kind of pump may be a waste of your money. This pump really is not adequate to maintain a milk supply. In this category, some good options include the Medela Single Deluxe and the Avent Isis IQ Uno.

• A personal double electric breastpump. Although they are more expensive – anywhere from $200 - $375, the investment is well worth it. You will be saving far more than that amount when you don't have to buy formula. Furthermore, the continued antibody protection of your breastmilk will keep your baby healthier and save you money on doctors' bills. The big advantage to these pumps is that you are able to pump both breasts at the same time, which actually increases your prolactin levels as well as reducing your pumping time. Good options include the Spectra S1 or S2, the Luna Motif and the wearable Elvie Stride. Some of these incorporate two-phase expression. At the beginning the suction is rapid and shallow, just like a baby when he first latches on. Then once your milk lets down it changes to a deeper more intermittent suction.

• A hospital-grade pump. Ameda and Medela are the two most widely-known manufacturers of hospital-grade breastpumps. These pumps are the best solution for the mother who is trying to maintain a complete milk supply when she cannot breastfeed at all. They offer the most stimulation and are best able to empty the breast. You can rent one of these pumps by the week or by the month. The Medela Symphony pump also offers the state-of-the art Two-Phase Expression technology. This feature makes the Symphony the ideal pump for moms who really need to maintain a good supply. However, since it is a hospital grade pump, it is cost-prohibitive for most mothers to purchase. To find the Medela rental station closest to you, go to http://www.medela.com/scripts/dealer_locator.htm For an Ameda dealer go to https://www.ameda.com/product_locator

Quick tips for a successful pumping experience

Once you have found the right pump, you need to get comfortable using it. Practice with it before you have to go back to work.

It is a very good idea to begin pumping several weeks before your return to work so that you can get some milk stored up. Remember that if you want your baby to take a bottle, it is important to introduce it to him as soon as breastfeeding is well established - some time toward the end of the first month of his life.

For some women, successful pumping really depends on emotional and psychological factors. Remember that the hormone adrenaline interferes with oxytocin, so try to avoid stress and anxiety. The following hints may help you pump more successfully:

• Before pumping, apply warm compresses to your breasts and use breast massage to help induce let-down.

• Have a picture of your baby where you can see it as you pump, or make a recording of your baby's sounds.

• Consciously relax when you are pumping. You might want to use this time to memorize Scripture. Having verses posted where they pump helps some women.

You've Gotten it Out – Now Put it Away!

You want to make sure that you store your liquid gold properly so that it will be of maximum use to your baby. All of the major breastpump companies make special bags for storing your breastmilk. The Medela bags, for example, work beautifully with Medela pumps because you can pump directly into the bag. This is really the easiest way to store your milk. However, breastmilk collection kits are available, as well. You can pump into a traditional bottle and store your milk in the bottle. If you are pumping today what baby will be using tomorrow, this might be the best, most economical system for you. However, if you are stocking up for future use, then the bags might be a better option. Be sure that you always label each bag with the date the milk was collected. When you use stored milk, remember the "first in, first out" principle: the first milk you put in the freezer is the first milk you take out when you need to use stored milk.

The following guidelines will help you decide how to store your milk.

- Fresh breastmilk should be used within 4-6 hours.

- Refrigerated breastmilk should be used within 3-5 days.

- Milk stored in the freezer compartment of a refrigerator/ freezer should be used within 4-6 months.

- Milk stored in a deep freeze should be used within a year.

TAKING CARE OF YOURSELF

Whether you have a job outside of the home or spend all day taking care of your baby, one thing is certain: you must make time to take care of yourself. Women who work all day, then come home to care for a baby, and husband and the home which houses them all, can quickly become burned out. Be sure that your husband reads this section, too, so he will be reminded again how important it is for you to spend time in the very worthwhile endeavor of taking care of YOU!

Sally has three children, 8, 4 and 7 months She also works a part-time job from her home. Recently Sally was at the point of absolute burn-out. She felt like she had nothing left to give to her children, her job or even her husband. When she opened up with her mom's group about her frustration, almost every mother in the group had experienced the same thing at one time or another. A couple of the moms offered to take Sally's kids for an afternoon so Sally could go out alone and enjoy a good book by herself. After her alone time, Sally felt somewhat rejuvenated.

Don't be afraid to ask for help from friends or relatives when you need a break from everything. While you probably won't want to take an overnight trip without your baby, you can still sneak in some time for you. Take a look at the following list and see what you can do to battle Mommy burn-out.

- Go to the bookstore alone for a couple of hours

- Treat yourself to a few hours at a day spa

- Go shopping with your best girlfriend (without your babies)

• Have a girl's evening out at your favorite restaurant – get dressed up and let your hubbies keep the kids.

• Choose a romantic comedy and as soon as baby is asleep pop some popcorn and have a date with your husband.

Always remember that this season of life is truly fleeting. Before you know it, these days will be nothing more than a fond memory. When you feel like you are overwhelmed by all your obligations, take a deep breath and remember, "I can do all things through Christ who strengthens me." Phil. 4:13.

Chapter 12:

"Bretiquitte" –
Some Advice on Nursing in Public

So whether you eat or drink or whatever you do, do it all for the glory of God.

– I Corinthians 10:31

Amy sat in the children's museum quietly nursing her infant using a blanket to cover herself as her toddler explored nearby when a museum worker approached her. "Would you please go to the bathroom to do that?" he asked. Offended because she didn't want to feed her baby in a public restroom (would you want to eat lunch in one?), Amy took action, launching an initiative that became Alabama state law in July of 2006. The law simply states that, "A mother may breastfeed her child in any location, public or private, where the mother is otherwise authorized to be present."

Across the country states are passing much-needed laws that give women the right to breastfeed in public. Opponents are quick to criticize nursing mothers for exposing themselves. However, I've never met a single breastfeeding mother who was trying to expose herself when she nursed. Nevertheless, as Christians, we do want to be modest and to avoid putting others in an uncomfortable situation. Remember that even as you feed your baby, you are doing it for God's glory!

NURSING DISCREETLY

Mary came into our store looking for a pump and some good bottles. As we discussed her situation, she explained that she wanted to pump milk so she could go out with her baby. She didn't think she would ever nurse in public because she is an extremely modest person. I understood exactly how she felt. Like Mary, I've always been very concerned about modest necklines. Nevertheless, as we talked about her options, she began to realize that she really could take her baby out with her and not have to have bottles to feed him.

Before you take baby out and try to nurse in public, you do need to make sure that you have breastfeeding well established, and both you and baby are comfortable with your nursing relationship. A wide variety of options are available for breastfeeding mothers who want to nurse discreetly. You need to figure out what works best for you and your lifestyle.

The Clothing Solution

A wide variety of stylish clothing is available for breastfeeding mothers. Some designers make clothing appropriate for both pregnancy and breastfeeding. Japanese Weekend, for example, has a "During and After" line which is quite stylish. Some mothers, however, may feel that the necklines on some pieces are too low. You need to find a local retailer so that you can actually try each piece on instead of just ordering on-line. When you try on a nursing top, make sure that the opening works for you. There are many different styles of openings, and some work better than others, depending upon your breast size.

Another option which is growing in popularity is the Bella Band (http://www.bellaband.com/bellaband.html). The concept here is really quite simple. It is a wide band that is worn over the top of the pants or skirt and provides coverage from the waist up to the bra line. It looks like you're wearing a t-shirt underneath your shirt, and allows you to nurse more discreetly in any shirt.

Of course, you need to make sure that your nursing bra fits well and is easy to use, too. Have someone who is trained in fitting nursing bras measure you and check the fit. Remember when you try on your nursing bra to use the "bend and scoop" technique. Bend over from the waist and scoop all of your breast tissue into the bra. See how easy it is to open and close the cups. Ideally you want a bra that you can open with one hand. Bravado and Glamourmom both make a nursing tank that has a full support bra built in. A nursing tank layered under another shirt is a great option for discreet breastfeeding.

Covering Up

Many mothers look for a way to cover themselves up while they are nursing. A wide variety of products are available on the market. Google "nursing covers" and you will find a variety of styles from which to choose. The basic blanket has taken on a new twist with the advent of Hooter Hiders (http://www.bebeaulait.com/) These stylish and practical nursing covers look like an apron with an adjustable neck strap. They provide enough room for even an older baby to nurse discreetly and comfortably, without making him feel too confined. Modest Mums (http://www.modestmums.com/) offers a very similar product.

Nursing tanks are a terrific option for moms on the go. You can wear it under almost any shirt in your wardrobe and have an instant modest nursing shirt! Bravado has wonderful tanks, but you can even find less expensive tanks at Target and WalMart.

Wearing your breastfed baby

Baby slings have enjoyed a tremendous surge in popularity. An explosion of companies producing chic baby carriers has created a buzz even in Hollywood where celebrity moms showcase their newborns in the trendiest slings around. Honestly, the most important thing in choosing a baby carrier is your comfort.

Ring slings like the Maya Wrap (www.mayawrap.com/) are adjustable and allow you to pull your baby in closer when you need to. The Maya Wrap has a nice long tail that you can use to cover yourself more fully. You can find a wonderful list of various types of slings here: https://www.thebump.com/a/baby-ring-slings

Pouch slings like the Peanut Shell (www.goo-ga.com) and Hotslings (www.hotslings.com) are less bulky than traditional ring slings, but not as deep. It is very important that you have the correct fit with a pouch sling. The lowest point of the sling should sit between your naval and your hip bone. Your baby should fit snugly in the sling. It can be very dangerous to wear a baby in a sling that is too big! Make sure to watch a video or have someone teach you how to use a sling when you first get started!.

Many other varieties of baby carriers exist. From the Baby K'tan wrap to soft structured carriers like Tula, many options are available. However, I have found that mothers have a more difficult time breastfeeding in non-sling types of carriers. If you are looking for a way to wear your baby that is most compatible with breast-feeding, by all means get a sling!

What if Someone Notices?

Despite your best attempts to maintain your modesty, someone may say something to you at some point about nursing in public. Maybe nothing is showing, but baby's delightful sounds make it obvious that she's busy getting her tummy full at your breast. Some people might really be offended at the thought that you would nurse your baby – discreetly or not – in public. How should you respond?

Of course, your first responsibility is to maintain a Christ-like attitude. You don't want to give offense, even when offense has been given to you. Nevertheless, you have a legal right to provide nourishment for your baby anywhere. Laws vary from state to state, but in most places, you cannot be asked to leave an establishment simply because you are nursing. You can find the specific law pertaining to your state at the following website: www.ncsl.org/programs/

health/breast50.htm. Furthermore, a 1999 amendment added to a postal appropriations bill states that a woman may breastfeed her child in any federal building where she otherwise has the right to be. (www.llli.org/llleaderweb/LV/LVJunJul05p51.html)

When someone makes a negative comment about your breast-feeding, or asks you to leave, be polite in your response. However, if you know that you have a legally protected right to breastfeed, you do not have to leave or stop nursing. Some mothers actually carry a copy of their state's law with them at all times for this very purpose.

What if it happens at church? You're sitting toward the back, quietly nursing your baby in a sling, and someone expresses dis-approval. As long as your baby isn't making a lot of noise and your skin isn't exposed, you really aren't causing any kind of disruption at all. Some people (especially older ones) are really set in their ways. Perhaps their generation didn't breastfeed very much, and they just don't understand it. Take the time to gently engage your critic in conversation, listening to her point of view, then carefully pointing out God's incredible design for infant feeding. You might even show her this book! Your goal isn't to win an argument; rath-er, it is to gently show the truth.

Chapter 13:

This Isn't How I Thought It Would Be –
Working Through Difficult Situations

Praise be to the God and Father of our Lord Jesus
Christ ... who comforts us in all our troubles, so
that we can comfort those in any trouble with the
comfort we ourselves have received from God.

– II Corinthians 1:3-4

Amy and Chris George (I've used their real names here with permission) were overjoyed about the upcoming birth of their twin daughters. Both had visible roles in the community: Amy as a news anchor on a local television station, and Chris as a professional athlete. However, when Amy was only 19 weeks pregnant, something went dreadfully wrong. Life as she knew it came to a screeching halt as she was placed in the hospital on complete bed-rest. She remained there, hooked up to monitors for seven weeks before her baby girls entered the world fourteen weeks too early.

Melissa was born first, weighing only one pound, nine ounces. Ann Catherine followed at one pound, fifteen ounces. Melissa had fought to hang on for the seven weeks in Amy's womb, but she could fight no longer and passed away just two and half hours after her birth. Ann Catherine, however, survived and has grown into a beautiful young woman!

Amy's expectations for motherhood certainly never included spending hours pumping her breasts to provide optimal nutrition for a baby in the Neonatal Intensive Care Unit (NICU) of Huntsville Hospital for Women and Children. She never dreamed how this experience would change not only her family, but the entire focus of her life. She and Chris created the Melissa George Neonatal Memorial Fund at Huntsville Hospital Foundation to raise money for much-needed NICU equipment at the hospital where her girls were born. Eventually, Amy left her job as a news anchor (much to the disappointment of her many fans) to focus more fully on her fundraising efforts for the hospital. Working with the Huntsville Hospital Foundation, she has raised enough money to purchase five state-of-the-art infant beds for the NICU.

You probably have certain expectations for your baby's birth and how your baby will be. Every day you may pray for the safety of the little one you are carrying. You may picture how sweet it will be to have her nuzzled up to your breast contentedly feeding. However, sometimes the unexpected does happen, and your birth doesn't end up the way you planned it, or your baby has a condition that makes breastfeeding very challenging. You can overcome those obstacles, though and still give your baby the gift of your milk.

Prematurity

Any baby born before 37 weeks gestation is considered premature. Babies who are born between 34 and 37 weeks of pregnancy are considered "near-term" infants. However, they often have a great deal of difficulty nursing, even when they weigh over five pounds.

Prematurity can happen for a variety of reasons. Sometimes a mother develops a condition called toxemia, or pre-eclampsia, in her last trimester. Her blood pressure is elevated, her urine contains protein, and she may experience significant swelling of the face and hands. Left untreated, pre-eclampsia can lead to seizures and convulsions, and even death on rare occasions. Treatment will involve bedrest and medication. However, if the condition continues to progress, the baby will have to be delivered.

Other maternal factors may also lead to prematurity. An incompetent cervix begins to open before it is time for the baby to be born. Again, bedrest may help delay the premature birth, but may not completely prevent it. Mothers who have chronic illnesses may be at risk for preterm labor, as well. A Group B streptococcus infection (vaginal or urinary tract) could also lead to prematurity. Frequently mothers who are carrying more than one baby also struggle to carry their infants to term.

Certain other factors can cause premature delivery, as well. An early rupture of the amniotic sac surrounding the baby can force a mother to deliver too early. The placenta can begin to pull away from the uterine lining too early (placental abruption) or it may be lying too low in the uterus for the mother to be able to safely go to term (placenta previa). Sometimes the placenta ceases to function way too early, so the baby must be delivered if he is to have any chance of survival.

We do know certain things about premature babies and breast-feeding:

• Expressing your milk is the one thing you can do that will make a significant difference for your baby right now. The doctors and nurses are busy taking care of all of his medical needs, but only you can provide him with food that will be easy for him to digest and will help to keep him healthy. Don't ever underestimate the importance of your role!

• The milk of a mother who delivers her baby preterm is slightly different in composition than the mother of a term baby. It has higher levels of certain antibodies that help to keep the premature baby healthy. Premature infants who receive breastmilk have significantly fewer episodes of necrotizing enterocolitis (NEC) an intestinal inflammation that may lead to death and often requires surgical intervention.

• Many researchers suggest that the breastmilk given to a premature infant be fortified with additional protein and minerals. Studies have shown that premature infants are able to grow at a healthier rate when the milk is fortified. Human milk fortifiers are added to breastmilk in most US facilities.

• Skin-to-skin contact with the mother (kangaroo care) provides important stimulation to the premature infant. It also offers important psychological benefits for the mother. Some researchers note that mothers who are able to offer kangaroo care to their preemies have greater success with pumping.

• It is essential that a preemie be able to coordinate sucking, swallowing and breathing in order to successfully feed at the breast. Many facilities require that the infant be able to demonstrate this on a bottle before going to the breast. However research indicates that infants who go first to the breast and then to the bottle actually have fewer episodes of apnea and are better able to maintain heart rate, respirations and body temperature than infants who are first given the bottle. (Meier and Anderson)

Pumping for your preemie

Most NICU units have an IBCLC who is specially trained to help nursing mothers. You will probably be provided with a hospital-grade electric breastpump to use when you are at the hospital. Most facilities will make rental pumps available for you to use at home. The Medela Symphony pump with its two phase expression is really the ideal pump to establish and maintain your supply. The following tips will help as you pump for your preemie:

• Begin pumping within the first 24 hours after birth. Ideally, you will want to pump as soon as you are able to.

• Pump at least 8 times every 24 hours. You will space your daytime pumping sessions every 2- 2 ½ hours, and you will need to get up at least once during the night to pump.

• Always wash your hands thoroughly with soap and hot water before beginning. You don't want to accidentally make your tiny newborn sick!

• Keep a picture of your baby near you when you pump, or better yet, gaze at your baby or even have him kangarooed between your breasts as you pump. This will help you psychologically focus on him and not on the mechanics of pumping.

• Use warm compresses and breast massage prior to pumping in order to help your milk to let-down.

• Sometimes it helps to take a cleansing breath before pumping, and then use relaxation techniques to help the hormones responsible for breastfeeding do their job. If you are tense, you will produce adrenaline which inhibits oxytocin, the hormone responsible for let-down.

• Be careful to follow your hospital's guidelines for collecting and storing your breastmilk.

• Babies younger than 32 - 34 weeks will usually be fed by a nasogastric tube. Letting them suck on a pacifier during feeding may help them learn to associate a full tummy with the sensation of sucking. Ideally during this time, infants should spend as much time as possible in skin-to-skin contact with the mother. Gradually, they should be given the opportunity to smell and lick the nipple.

Usually by 34 weeks preemies are able to begin to learn to feed at the breast. Some researchers suggest that initial attempts should be done on a breast that has just been pumped. While baby may get a little milk, she won't experience the full force of let-down and milk squirting from several nipple openings at once. As baby learns to suck and swallow, she can progress to taking an entire feed at the breast. Many practitioners now believe that it is completely unnecessary to give a breastfed preemie a bottle. In fact, research indicates that premature infants actually respond better overall to feeds at the breast (Meier and Anderson).

By the time you are ready to take your newborn home, he should be able to receive nearly all of his nutrition at your breast. If he does need to be supplemented, however, your have a couple of options. After feeding, you might give him a prescribed amount of formula by cup or syringe. If you do have to supplement, be sure to pump your breasts after feeding to insure that they are receiving sufficient stimulation to produce the quantity of milk you need. Another option available to you is to give him the supplement at your breast using a feeding tube system (Lact-aid or Supplemental Nursing System.) This option allows him to receive all feeds at the breast, and also provides increased stimulation to your breasts as he feeds.

SICK BABY

Every mother dreams that her baby will be a healthy, beautiful little cherub. Most babies are. However, some babies are born with congenital conditions that make feeding difficult. Other babies develop illnesses that provide extra challenges. You might have to learn to deal with one of the following situations.

Cleft lip and/or palate

The severity of the condition and the location of the cleft will have a lot to do with a mother's success in nursing a baby who has a cleft. If just the lip is cleft, it may be possible for the baby to latch on in such a way that he can still get enough suction to nurse. There have been instances where a mother has been able to feed a baby with a complete cleft palate and bilateral cleft lip by allowing her breast to fill the area of the cleft. An obturator is a device made by a dentist to cover the cleft and allow the infant to nurse more effectively.

Congenital heart defects

When an infant is diagnosed with a heart defect at birth, his mother may not be able to feed him for 24 – 48 hours. However, it is critical that she establish a good supply as rapidly as possible. According to the American Heart Association, breastfeeding is actually easier on an infant with a heart defect than bottle feeding (http://www.americanheart.org/presenter.jhtml?identifier=3017976). However, it may be necessary to feed this infant more frequently because he may tire more quickly at the breast. If surgery is required, the immunological properties of breastmilk will help reduce the risk of any infection.

Downs syndrome

These babies can be breastfed, but often have poor muscle tone and require extra support. A baby with Downs syndrome will do better when he receives frequent stimulation from his parents touching him, feeding him and playing with him. Furthermore, learning to coordinate the tongue movements to breastfeed correctly may help promote better speech and language coordination later on.

Gastroesophageal reflux disease (GERD)

Some babies have a very difficult time keeping food down. Or they may seem especially fussy shortly after eating. If your baby is diagnosed with GERD, he will probably be placed on medication which will help significantly. Try nursing him in a more vertical position and placing him to sleep with his head slightly elevated.

Hydrocephalus

This condition usually requires surgery shortly after birth to place a shunt for drainage. Because of the weight of the baby's head, it may be nearly impossible to hold him for feeds. However, with the help of a lactation consultant, you may be able to feed lying down. The abundance of antibodies provided by breastmilk will help fight off infection when the shunt is inserted, so breastfeeding is especially important.

Jaundice

Produced by high levels of unconjugated bilirubin in the infant's blood, this condition is often marked by lethargy. A mother must work diligently to stimulate a baby with jaundice to nurse. Skin-to-skin contact is essential. Often the baby's physician will insist that he receive supplemental feeds. When this happens, the best way to get the supplement to the baby is through a feeding tube device at the breast.

Robin Sequence

This diagnosis involves several specific conditions that make breastfeeding virtually impossible.

Rely on your lactation consultant

Whatever situation you face with your sick newborn, your most important resource is a good lactation consultant. An IBCLC has been trained to deal with a wide variety of breastfeeding situations. She will know what techniques would work best for your specific situation. It is well worth the cost of the consult. Your insurance provider might even reimburse you for part of the visit. Be sure to ask your lactation consultant for a lactation "superbill" which has the insurance codes on it.

SICK MOMMY

Certain maternal heath conditions can also affect breastfeeding. You may have a pre-existing condition which requires special care when nursing, or the circumstances of your pregnancy and birth may make you unable to feed your baby temporarily. Either way, it can be emotionally devastating when you've hoped for an easy breastfeeding experience.

Diabetes Mellitus

A mother with insulin dependent diabetes mellitus (IDDM) has already experienced a high-risk pregnancy. Protocol in some hospitals still dictates that the infant be taken to a special care unit for observation immediately. This is actually counterproductive (Engleking and Page-Lieberman, 1986). Colostrum is key to stabilizing the infant's blood sugar. Furthermore, the practice of separating mother and baby often leads to reduced milk production for diabetic women. During the first weeks of breastfeeding, the mother must be very closely monitored for blood glucose levels. However, once breastfeeding is established, the mother may actually need to reduce her insulin intake by about one-fourth. When she weans, she will also need to carefully monitor her glucose levels.

Multiple Sclerosis

Pregnancy can be a wonderful time of remission for the woman with multiple sclerosis. However, in the first three months following birth, symptoms may not only return, but temporarily increase dramatically. Breastfeeding is not contraindicated for the mother with MS. However, she needs to check with her doctor or lactation consultant before she resumes her medication if she is nursing. Dr. Jack Newman does say that the interferon molecules are simply too big to be excreted into breastmilk, so the use of interferon should not be a contraindication to breastfeeding. Nevertheless, being a mother is exhausting, so a mother with MS should make it a priority to have household help in the early months.

Polycystic Ovarian Syndrome

Women with this condition may have difficulty getting pregnant. However, they also seem to have problems maintaining an adequate milk supply. The same drugs which help mothers sustain a pregnancy, progesterone and metformin, may also help them maintain lactation. The progesterone given during pregnancy helps with the glandular development necessary for lactation. Metformin is recommended for use throughout lactation. However, some women still have problems. Two herbal galactagogues, Goat's Rue and Fenugreek have also been helpful for some mothers. Motherlove makes a product called More Milk Special Blend that has been used with some success by mothers with PCOS.

Postpartum Depression

About 20% of women experience mild to moderate depression after childbirth, and another 70% experience the "blues" around the third day postpartum. If you find yourself crying constantly, unable to sleep, and feeling like you simply can't cope with motherhood, you really need to see your doctor. According to Thomas Hale, author of Medications in Mother's Milk the best antidepressants for breastfeeding mothers are Zoloft and Paxil, both of which are excreted minimally in breastmilk.

Viral illness

A common respiratory or intestinal virus hits every mother at some point. When you get a virus, your body immediately begins to produce antibodies to it. Breastfeeding while you are sick actually helps to protect your baby. He may get a touch of the virus, but it won't be nearly as severe as it would have been if he hadn't nursed and received some immunity.

Hepatitis

Several strains of hepatitis exist. According to Dr. Nancy Wright, there is no evidence of transmission of Hepatitis A through breastmilk. Infants born to mothers with Hepatitis B should receive Hepatitis B immune globulin (HBIG) and Hepatitis B vaccine; they can then safely nurse. When a mother has Hepatitis C, she needs to monitor her HCA-PCR levels. As long as they are negative, she should be able to nurse safely. As long as her infant has received the HBIG and Hepatits B vaccines, a mother with Hepatitis D can safely breastfeed.

HIV

There is about a 1 in 7 risk of HIV transmission from mother to infant through breastfeeding. In developed countries, the prevailing wisdom is that as long as a mother has access to breastmilk substitutes, she should not breastfeed. Nevertheless, in third world nations where access to safe breastmilk substitutes may be limited, breastfeeding may actually save lives, despite the risk of HIV transmission.

UNEXPECTED DEATH

One of the most difficult experiences imaginable is loosing a child. Children are supposed to bury their parents, not the other way around. Parents who suffer through the death of a baby grieve on a variety of levels. They grieve the loss of their baby; they grieve the loss of their dreams for the future; they grieve over the empty nursery. Walking past that door and knowing the cradle is empty causes a deep, empty ache in a mother's soul.

Prenatal death

She's seen her baby's heartbeat. She knows he's a boy. She's felt his little butterfly kicks. Then suddenly the motion stops. The nagging fear that something is wrong becomes a heart-wrenching sob when an expectant mother finds out that her unborn baby has died. A miscarriage before the baby is viable is painful; but when a baby is close to his due date, the loss leaves a palpable empty space. After delivering the baby, her milk may come in on the third or fourth day causing her physical discomfort that only augments her suffering.

Stillbirth

Sometimes something goes wrong at the last minute and a baby is born dead or dies shortly after birth. The grieving mother should have the opportunity to hold him and experience the deep bonding that takes place between mother and child. However, she will ache at the thought that she will never get to know this precious little person. Regardless of the reason for his death, the sorrow is devastating. When her milk comes in a day or two after his funeral, her throbbing pain may very well be both physical and emotional. Some mothers may find comfort in donating their breastmilk to a milkbank program (see www.breastmilkproject.org for more information).

Death of a child

Whether the cause is SIDS, an illness, a congenital birth defect, or an accident, the loss of a baby or toddler is overwhelming. No parent should have to experience this, yet every day parents do face this unspeakable loss. Parents have had a chance to fall in love with this wonderful little person who has become an indispensable part of her life. They can't imagine life without him. Yet suddenly they are thrust into that reality: a lifetime without the child whom they love so deeply. When a mother is nursing the child who dies, she is faced with the cruelest and most abrupt of all weaning scenarios.

Dealing with your milk supply

The nursing mother who is faced with the sudden loss of her baby, whether through miscarriage, stillbirth, or death must find a way to dry up her milk supply. She should wear a bra that fits well but doesn't bind her breasts. Some mothers do prefer to use an Ace bandage binder. She may pump for comfort, but pumping too much can actually make the situation worse by stimulating milk production. Cabbage has an enzyme that actually helps reduce the milk supply, so she should wear cold cabbage leaves inside her bra, changing them every couple of hours. Crushing the veins in the leaves before applying them will release the enzymes. Sage is a great herbal remedy that will help to reduce milk supply. Taking sage capsules or extract 3 or 4 times a day will also help reduce the discomfort of full breasts.

Challenging situations will arise when you are a parent. Nothing is quite as challenging as losing a child. Nevertheless, your Heavenly Father understands even that pain. Knowing that you will see that precious child again one day provides hope. When King David's infant son was dying, he wept and mourned. Yet once the child had died, David accepted the fact and recognized that he would one day see him again in eternity. Cling to that precious hope with all your being!

Chapter 14:

Mary Treasured These Things in Her Heart –
Some Final Thoughts

*But Mary treasured up all these things and pon-
dered them in her heart.*

– Luke 2:19

Mary saw the mystery of the Messiah's birth unfold in unbeliev-
able circumstances. First, she became pregnant in an unprecedent-
ed supernatural event. Then just when it looked like her beloved
Joseph didn't want her anymore, an angel told him to go ahead and
marry her. Late in her pregnancy she had endured an exhausting
trip and gone into labor without the comfort of a familiar home-
town midwife. Finally, the peaceful birth scene had become quite
busy as shepherds came rushing in to see her new baby whom the
angels had called the Savior, the long-awaited Messiah.

Surely the next morning she must have wondered if it had all
been a dream. But when she looked down at her newborn son nuzzled next to her warm breast, she knew that this was no dream. No,
this was the unfolding of God's incredible plan for the ages. And

she was part of that plan! What inexpressible joy must have filled her at that realization.

You aren't Mary, and your baby isn't destined to be the Messiah. However, just like Mary, you and your newborn both have a special role to fill in God's plan. Your child may grow up to become a minister who will lead many to the Lord, or a singer whose voice will reach millions with the Gospel, or maybe a missionary who will spend her life ministering to a tiny group of people in a Third World Country. Or perhaps your child might become a teacher, a doctor, a police officer, a writer, an electrician, a factory worker, or a warehouse supervisor, and almost certainly a parent. The truth is that you have no idea today what God's plan is for this precious new life. But you can be sure of one thing: this baby was made to know Christ and be known by Him. You can do several very important things to encourage your child's faith from infancy on.

THREE KEYS TO MOTHERING

What is it that makes a woman a good mother? I'm sure if you addressed this question to ten different mothers, you would get that many different answers. However, as we look at mothers in the Bible and evaluate the way our Heavenly Father treats us, several principals emerge.

First of all, it is definitely NOT breastfeeding that makes you a good mother. Many wonderful mothers have not breastfed for one reason or another. But they have still been loving mothers who prayed for their children and cared for them with great tenderness. They are women who understood the importance of the following three principles:

• Love your child unconditionally.

• Build a lifelong relationship of trust with your child beginning in infancy.

• Pray without ceasing for your child.

We will examine each of these in the coming pages.

Love Your Child Unconditionally

Regardless of how badly we mess things up, God's love for us, His children, is absolutely unconditional. We can't do anything good enough to make him love us more. Nor can we do anything bad enough to make God stop loving us. He loves us because we are His, and he has chosen to call us His own.

> *For he chose us in him before the creation of the world to be holy and blameless in his sight. In love he predestined us to be adopted as his sons through Jesus Christ, in accordance with his pleasure and will.*
> *– Ephesians 1:4-5*

When you first gaze at your precious baby, you will be filled with wonder. You may not marvel at his beauty, because quite frankly most newborn babies are just not that pretty. However, to you he will be just perfect. You won't be able to imagine not loving him with your whole being. As the amazement and newness wear off, and the crying begins, you may find yourself experiencing mixed feelings.

Many mothers go through a brief period of frustration where they feel completely inadequate to handle the incredible responsibility they've been given. This is absolutely normal. One of the great benefits of breastfeeding is that it fills your body with hormones designed to help you fall head over heels in love with your baby - even when you feel frustrated. The love you feel for your baby isn't because of anything he has done. You love him because he is YOURS TO LOVE!

As he grows and develops into a lovely little person, you will find yourself enjoying him more and more. However, parenting gets more challenging with each new stage. Your challenge is to continue to love him regardless of how he behaves or what he says.

A child who knows that he is loved not because of what he does, but because of who he is, is secure in that knowledge. Will he be perfectly behaved? No, of course not; he inherited your sinful nature! However, he will be secure in his knowledge of your love, and that will certainly have a positive affect on his behavior.

Build a lifelong relationship of trust with your child beginning in infancy

Trust is a two-way street in parenting: your child trusts you, and as he gets older, you trust him. Babies have only one way of communicating hunger, distress, fear, boredom, or any other kind of discomfort: they cry. An infant doesn't distinguish between wants and needs. If he feels hungry, he lets you know. If he is uncomfortable, he lets you know. If he is too cold or too hot, he lets you know. When you respond to his needs immediately, you are teaching him that he can trust you.

Some "parenting experts" have warned against spoiling your baby. You may hear advice like this: "Don't hold him too much; you'll spoil him," or "Don't pick him up when he cries; you'll spoil him." Is that true? Will you spoil your baby by picking him up or holding him? ABSOLUTELY NOT! The reverse is actually true. After all, what is spoiling? When fruit spoils, it goes bad. A spoiled child has learned that unless he pitches a fit, he won't get what he wants. If you pick your baby up at the first signs of distress, you are teaching him that he doesn't have to pitch a fit. If you carry him or hold him when he needs to be held, you are teaching him that his world is secure, so he doesn't have to carry on to get attention.

Even some well-meaning Christian authors teach parents to be careful about feeding on demand or picking up a crying baby. They talk about the dangers of allowing your baby to manipulate you, as if this little person has spent the last nine months inside of your womb plotting and planning ways to bend you to his little will. The truth of the matter is that your new little person isn't conscious of much else outside of his needs. When you, as a loving mother, are quick to meet those needs, he grows in his awareness of his secure environment.

Babies learn very quickly. In the first year of his life he will go from being a completely helpless, dependent newborn to being able to feed himself, walk alone, express emotions and have a deeply connected bond of trust with you. You want to do all you can to forge the deepest trust possible.

God has blessed mothers with wonderful hormonal cues that trigger maternal feelings and responses. When my oldest was a newborn I tried so hard to follow the advice in the books I had read, even though it went against everything inside of me to let her lie in her crib and cry. I hated it. Some nights while she was screaming in her crib in her room, I was on the other side of the wall in my room sobbing. It was completely unnatural. God had designed me to nurture her and meet her needs, but the books I had read told me that I mustn't spoil her or let her manipulate me. Those books were dead wrong.

When you build a relationship of trust with your child from the moment he is born, it makes parenting so much easier later on. As your children grow into adolescents, then adults, the foundations you have laid during infancy will help to shape their ability to trust you .

If I could change anything about the way I have parented, I would never, ever, ever have made Sarah "cry it out." As you embark on the journey of parenting, try to peer 13 or 16 years down the road. What kind of relationship do you want with your teenager? If you want a relationship built on a foundation of trust, then begin laying that foundation the day she is born. You won't ever regret it!

Pray without ceasing for your child

Nothing you do as a mother will have a more eternal impact than your prayers for your child. When you bring your offspring before the throne of grace again and again, you are better able to keep an eternal perspective on the day-to-day frustrations of parenting. Does praying diligently for your child automatically guarantee that she will always be the perfect child? Does it give you assurance that no harm will befall him? Unfortunately, it does not.

Nevertheless, your diligent prayers do directly affect your child in a couple of ways. First, they provide a kind of spiritual safety net to help protect your child from evil influences. When you are in constant communication with the Lord about your child, your own spirit will be more sensitive to influences that could harm him. From the earliest music and videos to preschool TV shows and beyond, some things your child sees and hears will be beneficial for him, but many will not. As you continually pray for your children, you will have a quickened sense of what may not be appropriate for him at a given stage.

Another effect of your diligent prayers is based on the Biblical truth that God answers prayer. When you pray for your child's salvation day by day, when you beseech the Lord to help your child develop godly character, your Heavenly Father hears those supplications. Ruth Graham has written about her fervent prayers for her rebellious son, Franklin. Although it took a while, Franklin turned from his rebellious lifestyle and became a leader in the evangelical world. Throughout Scripture we see examples of heavenly intervention in response to earthly prayers. God has a plan for your child, and He will be glorified in your child's life as you pray.

What about children who experience illness or other tragic circumstances? Does that mean their parents didn't pray well enough? Absolutely not. Remember the principle that God will be glorified in your child's life. Illness and tragedy are a consequence of original sin; none of us is exempt. However, as we bring even these difficult situations before God's throne, we will inevitably see the truth of Romans 8:28, "And we know that in all things God works for the good of those who love him, who have been called according to his purpose."

IN CONCLUSION

Pregnancy produces many emotions. You may be overjoyed, anxious, excited and scared all at the same time. Giving life to the next generation is an incredible privilege and an awesome responsibility. You will never be the same after you become a mother. Everything you do will in some way be affected by your baby. And you won't be able to imagine what life would be like without him!

Breastfeeding is clearly God's perfect plan for you and your baby. You both receive countless benefits as you feed her the way God intended you to. Nevertheless, you may encounter difficulties. Fortunately help is readily available in most places. Don't hesitate to ask for it. Nursing your baby should be a joyful experience for you, one you will treasure long after your milk has dried up.

Even if you only nurse a few weeks, you will know that you have given your baby the best possible start in life. Don't let a failed breastfeeding relationship keep you from enjoying every moment of your baby's infancy. Remember to love him, to meet his needs, and to pray for him. If you do those three things consistently, your baby will be blessed indeed!

APPENDIX A – INFANT FEEDING RECORD

Use the chart below to keep track of your baby's nursing and elimination patterns in the early newborn period. Note what time he begins and ends on each breast. You can also keep track of when he has a wet or dirty diaper. This will help you know for sure that he's getting what he needs. Feel free to copy this page as often as needed.

Day	Right Breast	Left Breast	Wet Diaper	Dirty Diaper

BIBLIOGRAPHY

The following resources provide interesting background for the material found in this book.

"BFHI USA: Implementing the Baby Friendly Hospital Initiative in the U.S." BFUSA, 2004. http://www.babyfriendlyusa.org/eng/index.html

Crenshaw, Jeannette T. Healthy Birth Practice #6: "Keep Mother and Newborn Together - It's Best for Mother, Newborn and Breastfeeding." Journal of Perinatal Education Vol.28, No.2, April 1, 2019, pp 108-115.

Engelking, Cm and Page-Lieberman, J. Maternal diabetes and diabetes in young children: their relationship to breastfeeding. Lactation Consultant Series (Unit 5). Garden City Park, NY. 1986. Avery Publishing Group, inc.

Freeman, Marc E.; Kanyicska, Béla; Lerant, Anna; and Nagy, György. "Prolactin: Structure, Function, and Regulation of Secretion." Physiological Reviews, Vol. 80, No. 4, October 2000, pp. 1523-1631. The American Physiological Society.

Gartner, Lawrence M. et al. "AAP Policy Statement: Breastfeeding and the Use of Human Milk." Pediatrics Vol. 115 No. 2 February 2005, pp. 496-506. http://aappolicy.aappublications.org/cgi/content/full/pediatrics;115/2/496

IBFAN/ICDC Penang. "Implementing the International Code." http://www.ibfan.org/english/pdfs/lwtdhiv01.pdf

Kelly, Carolyn Griffith. "PCOS and Breastfeeding." Breastfeeding Update. October 2003. San Diego County Breastfeeding Co-alition. http://www.breastfeeding.org/newsletter/v3i3

Kennedy KI, Rivera R and McNeilly AS. "Consensus statement on the use of breastfeeding as a family planning method." Contraception, 1989, 39(5):477-496

McKenna, James. "Sudden Infant Death Syndrome." Nov. 20, 2004. http://www.nd.edu/~jmckenn1/lab/articles/Cambridge%20 Handbook%20of%20Child%20Development.pdf

Meier, P., Anderson, G. "Responses of Small Preterm Infants to Bottle and Breast Feeding" The American Journal of Maternal Child Nursing. March, 1987. 12:97-105.

Mosko, S., Richard, C. and McKenna, J. "Maternal Sleep and Arousals During Bedsharing with Infants." Sleep. Vol. 20, No. 2 1997. pp.142-150. http://www.nd.edu/%7Ejmckenn1/lab/articles/C.pdf

Newman, Jack. "You Should Continue Breastfeeding." January, 2005. http://www.bflrc.com/newman/breastfeeding/still_bf.htm

Overton, Larry. "Breastfeeding and the Bible." 2001. http://www.texas-midwife.com/breastfeeding.htm#idiomatic

Riordan, Jan and Auerbach, Kathleen G. Breastfeeding and Human Lactation. Boston, MA. 1993. Jones and Bartlett Publishers, inc.

Sinusis, Keith, and Gagliardi, Amy. "Initial Management of Breastfeeding." American Family Physician. Vol. 64, No. 6, Sept. 15, 2001. pp. 981-988. http://www.aafp.org/afp/20010915/981.html

USDA/ARS Chidren's Nutrition Research Center at Baylor College of Medicine. "Fortified Breastmilk Best for Premature Infants." 2004 http://www.kidsnutrition.org/consumer/nyc/volfa-99b.htm

Wright, Nancy E., MD, FAAP, IBCLC. "Breastfeeding in High Risk Populations: The Mom with Hepatitis." Breastfeeding Update. December, 2001. San Diego County Breastfeeding Coalition. http://www.breastfeeding.org/newsletter/v1i4/

Made in USA - Kendallville, IN
15333_9780998488226
04.17.2024 1246